"*Doing What Matters* distills one of the most important aspects of running a successful business—building a practical framework for continual improvement—into a meaningful and compelling story. Readers will recognize themselves in Mike Spur and will enjoy joining Mike as he learns about the Learning Loop. The fundamentals of the process are underscored by another critical success factor: the need for excellent leadership. Concise and brisk, the story unfolds easily, and each page has something the reader will want to highlight, underline, and refer back to later."

—Jim Kasch, Canidae Consulting

"The concepts and ideas that John identified in the book truly resonated with me—specifically, the member/client-centric approach to organizational effectiveness."

—Gene Pelham, President/CEO, Rogue Credit Union

"The storyline is easy to follow and interesting, pulling you into the narrative and allowing you to become engaged in learning material. ... The characters are likable and relatable as people that we could be in the same situation as the story follows the drama of potential failure turned into success. It's a great pre-read for training, particularly for strategic or tactical training."

—Dr. Susan Cain, Corporate Learning Institute

"Throughout the book, anyone in any form of financial services will see examples that they will immediately recognize and will think of specific applications. I have a reading list that I've used for some years with a presentation on 'Principles for Credit Union Leadership.' That list is about to get an addition of *Doing What Matters*. Thanks, John, for your contribution to the financial services industry—and to many other business sectors as well!"

—John M. Tippets, Consultant, speaker, and retired credit union CEO

"I was able to apply the Learning Loop within the first day of reading *Doing What Matters*. I appreciated the emphasis on how vital it is to offer tools and coaching with care and concern to assist colleagues, how accountability is such a positive value, and how the Learning Loop can be a filter to stay focused on what's important to the business."

—Gary E. Ahlgren, Executive Vice President, USE Credit Union

Doing What Matters

How Leaders Help
Individuals
and Organizations
Thrive

John Janclaes

Published by The CEO Corner

www.theceocorner.com

Copyright © 2016 by John Janclaes

ISBN 978-0-9972186-0-2

Dedication

To those who embrace
the responsibilities of leadership

Contents

Preface

Learning to lead is a lifelong journey, one best traversed with others— mentors, colleagues, and fledgling executives just beginning their trek.

Throughout my twenty-five years as a business executive, I have seen the gains that result in the lives and careers of individuals and in the growth of organizations when leaders embrace their responsibility to champion the professional and personal development of their teams. As Edward Hallowell writes in his book *Shine*, "The more a manager can help the people who work for him or her to shine, the greater that manager will be, and the greater the organization as a whole. Put simply, the best managers bring out the best from their people" (Harvard Business Review Press, 2011, p. 2). I've benefited from this dynamic throughout my career, and I've sought to emulate and promote this approach in my own leadership roles, most recently as President/CEO of Partners Federal Credit Union.

The idea for this book first came to me during my tenth anniversary year with Partners, which serves employees of The Walt Disney Company. We had accomplished most of what we had set out to do during that decade, even amid an extended economic recession that was especially hard on California and Florida, our primary service regions. We had completed one of the largest mergers in credit union history, which helped us grow into one of the biggest credit unions in the country. In observance of this anniversary, I was interviewed for a trade journal article. One of the questions the editor asked was, "Which accomplishment are you most proud of during your tenure?" The answer was easy: Our credit union had transformed itself from a good organization into a thriving enterprise by Doing What Matters.

Putting that realization into words motivated me to harvest some of the lessons learned throughout my career, and so I began to review my personal journals. Journaling is a daily practice for me. A mentor introduced me to journaling nearly twenty-five years ago as a way to capture ideas that might improve my life and work. Over the years, I've created a library of more than forty journals filled with handwritten notes, sketches, and diagrams. I highly recommend journaling as part of a daily routine. In my experience, the return on investment of time and reflection has been staggering.

Pouring over the pages of my journals afforded me the opportunity to revisit personal and experiential milestones, evoking moments of joy and laughter and some tears as well. I also retraced the arc of my professional life to date, from my earliest aspirations through the setback of a layoff and then on and up through the ranks of several financial services companies. I had learned and accomplished a great deal over the decades, all with the support of family, friends, and business associates.

I had a lot to be grateful for, but I wanted to make this journey through memories more purposeful. My aim was to understand what enduring principles could be repurposed so that I might do more, serve more, contribute more, and experience more of what life has to offer, because these experiences made me feel alive. These explorations turned up much that I could apply to my future planning and to share with others. Captured in my journals were many enduring ideas, tools, and tenets that I had discovered, explored, and developed. Among the most valuable were entries in which I sought to identify and codify my life purpose, which might be summarized in these words:

> My purpose, every single day, is to be in sync with the natural rhythms of life, to create environments in which I and others can thrive and which would enable me to take action without knowing how things will work out, thereby living a life filled with adventure.

If a key aspect of my purpose is to help others and myself, how might I translate and share the principles and tools that helped me succeed in achieving my goals? That seemed to be a worthy challenge—and the genesis of this book, which unfolds as a story of a manager who falters but then finds his way with the guidance of caring and capable leaders. Though the characters are fictional, the framework developed within these pages captures the essence of the tenets at the center of my professional and personal life. Sharing these tenets in *Doing What Matters* is one way to fulfill my commitment to advocate for the role of leaders in championing the professional development of their managers and employees. Proceeds from sales of this book will go toward scholarships for training for future leaders.

In tandem with the publication of this book, I've launched The CEO Corner (www.theceocorner.com), an online forum to foster a supportive community for business leaders. The CEO Corner will feature insights on successful leadership, offered through C-Suite Interviews, featuring podcasts, blogs, and other content for executives across the business spectrum. As you read this book and begin applying and adapting the ideas presented here in your organization, I invite you to become a regular visitor and participant at The CEO Corner.

If you are ready, let's begin the journey to discover together how Doing What Matters is the foundation for leaders helping individuals and organizations to thrive!

John Janclaes

April 2016

Chapter 1

Promises to Keep

The crack of a bat connecting solidly with a baseball startles Mike Spur from his uneasy reflections.

Hunched over his desk at Tri Counties Insurance (TCI), Mike had been staring at the columns of the sales report until the numbers blurred and his thoughts jumbled gloomily. He welcomes the distraction of a game of sandlot baseball outside his open office window. The kids are taking advantage of a fine autumn evening in Rancho Santa Fe, California, making the most of their after-school hours. The fielders heckle and punch their fists into their gloves as the next batter steps up to the plate, kicks up a small puff of dust, and digs in for the first pitch. They are so engrossed in the game that they seem oblivious to the waning light until one of their mothers sounds the call for dinner. Only when her voice grows sharper and rings louder across the diamond do they reluctantly gather their gear and jog toward home.

Mike smiles at his own childhood memories of being so caught up in playing with his friends that the day would pass before they knew it. He forces his mind away from this pleasant distraction to focus on his cluttered desk. At this pace, he still has two hours of work to get through before he can head home. He rubs his forehead wearily at another thought: I used to love my work. I remember looking up with surprise when other people headed out the door at the end of the day. Where did that passion go?

Just then, Nikki strides by his open door. "Good night, Mike. Don't stay too late," she calls. His first thought is, yeah, yeah, followed by a tinge of professional jealousy. How could it be that Nikki can arrive each day at 8 a.m., leave at 5:30 p.m., and still be the top-producing agent in the office for three years running? He works so many more hours than she does that it doesn't seem fair.

As the sun sets, his view of the playground fades as the glazed windows become a mirrored wall, and Mike finds himself staring at his reflection. He tries to shake off his funk as he returns to the stack of manila folders he needs to review and sign off on before heading home. The files hold the promise of completed sales for the week, and he hopes there will be enough new accounts to meet his region's goal for the month. If not, Mike worries that his long-term relationship with his boss will suffer yet another blow. The last thing he needs is to miss sales projections for a third month in a row, but Mike knows this result is a very real possibility.

TCI is the second largest insurance agency in Southern California, serving Orange, San Diego, and Riverside counties. Its patriarch is Jim

McKinnon, who established the agency more than 20 years ago with his wife, Kate. Although Jim and Kate could sell the agency at a handsome profit, they've held on to it because they believe the agency serves the community and, just as importantly, gives its employees an opportunity to thrive. Established in Rancho Santa Fe, TCI enjoys its strongest foothold there in its home community. The company's greatest attribute is its recruitment, development, and promotion of talent. TCI's competitors spend a lot of time trying to deconstruct what Jim McKinnon set into motion two decades ago in an effort to learn the firm's "secret sauce."

Mike is one of the prodigies Jim recruited. He progressed smartly by working hard and being open-minded, advancing from top-producing agent to sales manager to his current role as Regional Vice President of the San Diego County region. His ascent to VP allowed Mike and his wife, Megan, to provide their children with advantages any parenting duo would be grateful for. Until the last few months, one of those advantages was a more predictable schedule that allowed Mike to spend more time with his family. Lately, though, he'd been logging long hours in his office even as sales in his region leveled off and then began declining—not a precipitous drop, but still frustrating and discouraging because the time he put in to managing his sales staff seemed fruitless, wasted.

"Mike, Mike, are you still here?" calls out Sammy, an old friend of the McKinnons who leases an office down the hall for his part-time business. "I heard Nikki tell you to call it a day."

"Yeah, yeah, she did," Mike grumbles. "I wish I could go home early, but I'm not a sales agent anymore who's only accountable for myself. I remember those days. I had so much freedom!"

"So ... what? You want to go back to being an agent? Really?"

"No, no. I know there's no going back, Sammy. Besides, being a sales agent is not compatible with being a father of two kids—with all those evening and Saturday appointments with policyholders. And the extra money I earn now surely helps." Mike pauses and sighs. "I just need another hour or so here. Good night, Sammy."

"Night, Mike. And say hello to Megan and the kids for me." As Sammy heads for the door, Mike can hear his footsteps echo down the hallway.

Mike turns back to the files on his desk. As he calculates sales, it becomes clear that his region will not meet its targets. Again. His thoughts race from bad to worse. First, he envisions the disappointed reactions of his direct boss Sean McCarthy and Mr. McKinnon, both of whom he respects and admires. Then, the possibility of continuing slipping sales commands his attention, and a wave of panic pours over him as he imagines losing his job. Just thinking about such a scenario drains his energy from head to toe. How could he ever tell Megan that he has failed?

The final tabulation of sales results shows that his region achieved 80 percent of target for the month, down a full 10 percent from the prior month. Mike reluctantly prints the report and places it in Sean's in-basket to be reviewed in the morning. Just after 7:30 p.m., Mike rolls into his driveway, and the headlights pierce the dark evening and bounce off the walls inside the house. Before Mike can even grab his briefcase and exit the car, the front door flies open and the kids bound off the porch toward him. "Daddy, Daddy!" calls 5-year-old Jake. His sister, Jessica, older by two years, is right behind him: "Hi, Dad. We waited dinner on you, but then Mom said we should eat so I could do my homework."

Mike hugs them both and looks up to see Megan's silhouette appear in the doorway. She waves them all in, and Mike stomps toward her with a giggling child hanging from each arm. He steps up on the stoop, kisses his wife, and says, "Sorry, hon, I know I should've been home earlier. I needed to finish up the sales report for Sean."

"And how are sales?" Megan asks.

"Not good. I really don't want to talk about it right now." Mike eats his dinner with Jessica next to him at the dinner table, going through her homework. Then he reads Jake a bedtime story. His son's favorite book of the moment is Dr. Seuss's *Horton Hatches the Egg*, in which an elephant keeps his promise to tend to an egg. Jake laughs at every picture of Horton precariously perched on a nest on a tortured tree limb, but his father is more pensive as he reads Horton's vow, "I meant what I said and I said what I meant. An elephant's faithful one hundred percent."

Mike is preoccupied as he settles in with Megan for a little TV after tucking the kids in. Even his favorite show does not distract him from his thoughts: I'm not doing a very good job of keeping my promises to Sean, to Mr. McKinnon, to Megan, Jessica, and Jake. And what about the promises I made to myself? I wish I knew what to do.

Chapter 2

Walk, Trot, Canter

After a fitful night, Mike heads back to the office Friday morning, dreading his conversation with his boss.

As soon as he enters the office, Mike is met with a stack of phone messages and warm "Good morning" from the office administrator, Jen, who quickly adds, "Sean is waiting in his office to go over the sales report. Good luck."

As Mike enters Sean's office, his boss's back is to him, and Mike can see that he is marking up the report. He searches his mind frantically for a moment, trying to come up with an explanation, but he settles for, "Good morning, Sean. I see you've got our numbers. What do you think?"

"Not so much," Sean replies, looking up at him. "Sales down 10 percent, and this is—what?—the third month running your region has been below target? What's going on?"

"I'm not sure," Mike says. "Honestly, I'm getting a little worried."

"Well, you're not the only one. Mr. McKinnon is getting worried, too. He called just before you came in to get an update on sales from each region, and I had to tell him that yours was the only one not on target."

Mike wonders briefly to himself if Mr. McKinnon has put it all together and realized that the disappointing sales results weren't just isolated but part of a trend. Of course he knows, Mike thinks. Mr. McKinnon always has his pulse on sales for every region. Sean's next words under-score that reality.

"Actually, Mike, Mr. McKinnon wants to see you this morning. He asked if you'd drive out to the house. Listen, I know you're probably freaking out right now, but try to take this in stride. Go see him and then come back to the office so we can discuss your conversation."

Driving down the Ortega highway toward Mr. McKinnon's home, which is really a ranch, Mike feels oddly relieved. His initial anxiety has given way to the knowledge that Mr. McKinnon has always been a fair man and a good mentor. Mike would rather talk with him face to face than worry endlessly about disappointing him and letting down the company he's worked so hard to build.

Arriving at the main gate of the ranch, Mike pushes the intercom button and is met with a warm and familiar voice welcoming him. "Jim is waiting for you out by the barn," Kate McKinnon says. "Just drive around back."

Before Mike can get out of car, the ranch's greeter is on the job. Roxy, the McKinnons' hound, barks and wags her tail excitedly, awaiting a pat on the head. Mr. McKinnon comes around the barn, alerted by Roxy, and approaches his visitor. "Good morning, Mike. Glad you could make it out. Get down, Roxy, come on. You can join us on our walk."

Mike takes a deep breath and falls in step with Mr. McKinnon. The barn is meticulous and buzzing with activity. A couple horses are on the hot walker, an exercise machine like a treadmill, while others stand in the cross-ties getting tacked up by grooms. Out in the arena, a few horse-and-rider teams are clearing jumps. The scent of Poet's Jasmine hangs over the scene. Mike feels the tension ease out of his shoulders a bit.

Mr. McKinnon looks out over the arena as they walk. "Do you know why I asked Sean to have you come see me this morning, Mike?"

"I think so. My region's sales are down—three months in row, and each month a little further from target than the last. I'm trying everything I know about managing a sales team, and nothing seems to be closing the gap. I have to admit that I've been a bit on edge and pressing the team really hard. Some of them seem burned out. I don't know, maybe it's time to get a new team."

Just then a horse and rider near a fence. As the horse jumps, it knocks down the top rail. Mr. McKinnon calls, "You never had that horse balanced and rode it too deep into the jump."

Then he turns his attention back to Mike. "You know, managing a high-performing sales team, any team, is about mastering a half-dozen things. In riding, those things are being able to balance the horse as you ride straight, turn left and right, and do that at three gaits, which are walk, trot, and canter."

The same rider approaches the fence and this time jumps it clean. "There you go!" cheers Mr. McKinnon. "Did you feel how well balanced you and the horse were as you approached the fence? Super job. That was real nice!

"See Mike, that team—the rider and the horse working together—cleared that fence because they performed as one on the things that really matter. I asked you to come out here today because I think I know why your team's sales have been down. I believe you've lost track of what really matters. And I want you to know that I am still your biggest champion. Your career as an executive is going to be very bright if we get you refocused on what matters.

"So here's what I would like you to do: Go back to the office and work with Sean and some of your colleagues there. He's assembled a good team, some of the most successful folks I know. All I ask is that you fully participate, stay open-minded, and try out some new behaviors. If you do that, I have tremendous confidence in your abilities. I think your team will be able to meet and exceed your sales targets, and I believe you'll discover your full potential. Can you do that?"

Mike shakes Mr. McKinnon's outstretched hand. "Thank you, sir," he says. "It means a lot to me that you still have confidence in me and are willing to champion my development."

Mr. McKinnon nods his head toward the arena. "Remember, Mike, focus on what matters—just like that team out there. Walk, trot, canter. Walk, trot, canter. Well, I'd better get after my chores. Have a good day, Mike, and I'll see you again soon."

Chapter 3

The Learning Loop

"You're right on time," Jen announces as Mike walks back into the office.

"On time for what?" he asks, mentally going over his schedule for the day to see if he's forgotten an appointment. Jen points down the hall to the conference room and tells him Sean and "the team" are waiting for him.

As Mike enters the conference room, he is greeted by Sean, Nikki, and a familiar-looking gentleman. As Mike struggles to put a name with the face, the man greets him, "Hello, Mike, we've met before but it's been awhile. I'm Phil Cummings. I was owner of the San Diego County Insurance Agency before Jim bought us out, oh, it must be seven years ago now. I think you had just come on board as a sales agent."

"Mr. Cummings, of course I remember you. Good to see you again." As he leans across the table to shake the older man's hand, Mike is trying to figure out the purpose of this meeting. If he's to be taken to task for his region's declining sales, why is Nikki here?

As if he senses Mike's hesitancy, Sean quickly steps in. "Mike, you're probably wondering why Jen steered you in our direction. Mr. McKinnon asked me to put together a coaching team to help you take your performance as a sales manager to the next level, and Nikki and Phil have graciously agreed to be a part of the team. So, should we get started?"

"Sean, hold on a minute. Have I done something wrong?" Mike asks. "I know sales are down lately, but every sales manager experiences a temporary downturn from time to time. This feels like ... I don't know ... an intervention or something."

"Well, I guess it is an intervention of sorts," Sean says. "I'll tell you what, if you can go to the whiteboard and outline what is going on and what needs to be done to get sales on track, we'll call it a day."

Sean hands Mike a dry ink marker, and Nikki and Phil each pick up a pen next to notepads in front of them as if they are prepared to take notes. Mike approaches the whiteboard, shifts the marker in his right hand, and raises his arm as if he is ready to write something. Instead, he pauses, his hand suspended in front of the board. A few seconds pass in silence, and then Mike sighs, drops his hand, and turns back to the team.

"Frankly, I have no clue why sales are down three months in a row," Mike admits. "Sure, I have one open position, and it's summertime so the agents are taking vacation just like our clients. But I also know our region has always posted strong sales during this time of the year, so that can't be it. At this point, I'm out of answers."

Immediately, he delivers a mental slap to his forehead. He thinks, I shouldn't have said that. Any sales manager who says "I don't have a clue" should probably be fired. But he also realizes that it's the truth.

"Mike, that's why we're here today," Sean says. "And right off the bat, you should know that this situation is not really unexpected."

"What do you mean?"

Sean takes the dry ink marker from Mike's hand and signals him to take a seat alongside Phil and Nikki. "OK, let's start with a review. Phil has a good memory. You did join the firm about seven years ago as a sales agent, and you quickly became one of the top-producing agents in the company. Then you took on an advisory role representing other agents' needs before becoming the best sales trainer I think we've ever had at TCI."

Sean continues to recap Mike's career with the company: About eighteen months ago, he was promoted to Regional Vice President in charge of sales for San Diego County, the company's largest region. Sales in that region increased month-over-month for twelve straight months after Mike was promoted, but then leveled off and began a steady decline. "Does that sound about right?" Sean asks.

"Yes, and it feels good to revisit some of my successes with TCI," Mike says, with just a hint of sarcasm. The others in the room nod, accepting his response as a sign that Mike is willing to open up about his current challenges.

"Mike, everyone here is your champion," Sean responds. "Among the four of us in the room, we've got almost seventy years of experience in the insurance business. Phil ran his own agency for more than forty years, so he has extensive expertise in both sales and operations. And Nikki is our top-producing agent for the last three years. In fact, her sales last year were more than the next three agents' combined. And I would like to think I bring something to the table as the leader who championed your promotion to sales manager and with my experiences as a regional sales manager for more than fifteen years."

Sean tells Mike that the team will be meeting over the next week for two to three hours each morning to review what he calls TCI's "secret sauce," a concept referred to within the company as the Learning Loop.

"That sounds familiar," Mike says.

"It might. For some of us at TCI, the lexicon and key concepts of the Learning Loop are guiding principles, something we refer to every day."

"Then why is this the first time I've heard about it in more than just a passing reference?"

"Have you ever heard the adage, 'The teacher appears when the student is ready'?" Sean asks. "We've found that it works better to learn from real experiences. Are you ready to start learning by doing?"

With this question, he slides open a panel that reveals another whiteboard displaying the depiction of the Learning Loop that someone had neatly transcribed (see Figure 3.1).

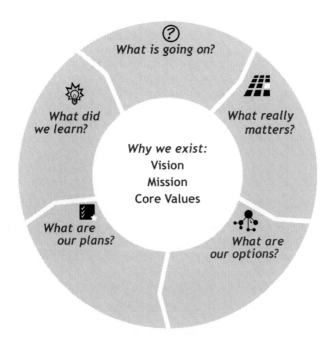

Figure 3.1 The Learning Loop

Sean explains that this will not be an academic exercise that takes place across the conference table. Instead, a series of discussions will be facilitated by short "field assignments" outside the office so that Mike has the opportunity to see the framework in action in different contexts and in interactions with a variety of people.

"Before you head out for your first little exploratory trip, let's look at this diagram," Sean continues. "The Learning Loop is a series of questions that you can ask and answer to reveal what matters in the context of what you're trying to do. In this case, we're trying to under-stand why and how your region's sales have declined after more than a year of success.

"So a useful foundation for the field interviews you'll be conducting might be to review the core mission of Tri Counties Insurance. Why does this company exist? What is our vision, and what are our core values?"

At this point, Phil picks up the discussion. "The day that Jim shared his mission for this company with me was the day I decided to merge my firm with TCI. He told me, 'We exist to help our policyholders thrive.' That's very different from a lot of other insurance companies—like Geico, for instance, which focuses on low rates. That's good for customers, too, but I really appreciated that Jim McKinnon wants to help his customers protect what matters most to them. That's an enduring mission, worth showing up for."

Because Phil maintains a small ownership share in TCI, he participated in the development of the company's vision statement and core values, which the team reviews next.

Vision statement: We exist to help our policyholders thrive—however they define it.

Mission statement: Tri Counties Insurance will insure the lives and/or the property of one in three households within our market areas (currently San Diego, Orange, and Riverside counties) by 2020. [The company currently holds policies with one in four households.]

Core values:

1. We treat others as we would like to be treated.

2. We champion what matters to our stakeholders.

3. We are accountable to one another for the results that drive the mission.

Mike looks around the table at the other three participants. "TCI does have a worthy mission, and the vision statement and core values certainly support it," he notes.

Sean nods in agreement. "And the significance of putting the mission, vision, and core values at the center of the Learning Loop is not a trivial thing. As we try to figure out what matters most from the many factors that arise in our daily business, we need to consider which of those factors harmonize with the core and which don't align. If they don't fit, then they're not options for our firm."

"I think of the core of the Learning Loop as a kind of filter," Nikki says. "That helps me narrow down a whole universe of options for the way I can do this job. For instance, I don't go in for a hard sell, but I am willing to spend as much time with clients as they need to sort through their options. I learned that in one of your training sessions, Mike."

"A filter—that's a good metaphor," Sean says. "Operating in today's business environment where there is so much going on, being able to figure out quickly what is in and what is out can be a differentiating capability, a real gift." Sean tells Mike that his first field assignment will be a trip with Nikki, who has set up several appointments for the rest of the day. Mike's first thought is the stack of folders on his desk, still awaiting his attention. His second is: Why Nikki? She's just an agent, and she just said she learned how to be a good one from me. He looks at the diagram of the Learning Loop for a moment, gives a small shrug, and thinks: I promised Mr. McKinnon I'd go into this with an open mind.

"Guess we'd better get started then," Mike says, rising from his chair.

Chapter 4

What Is Going On?

Before heading to the door to meet up with Nikki, Mike stops by his office to check for voicemail messages and then lets Jen know he'll be out for the day.

Jen tells him she's already received instructions from Sean: Let any callers for Mike know that he'll be back in his office the following afternoon.

On their way to Nikki's car, Mike asks, "So where are we headed?"

"To grab a cup of coffee with Maria Cortez," Nikki says.

"But ... wait. Maria works for the competition."

"Yup. She's the top sales agent for Southern California Insurance these days. We serve on a continuing education committee together, so when Sean asked me to line up a conversation with a successful sales agent, Maria was the first person I thought of."

Mike and Nikki meet Maria at Caffe Pasitano, a popular coffee shop well away from Maria's office. Without alluding to declining sales in Mike's division, Nikki simply tells Maria that they'd like to talk about her views on what makes a successful sales agent.

"Well, you should know—as the top agent for TCI," Maria says. "Not that I haven't tried to lure you over to our firm."

"And I've tried to talk you into moving to ours," Nikki says with a laugh. She adds more soberly, "That may be a good place to start. Maria, would you tell Mike why you wouldn't consider moving to TCI?"

"I actually did consider making the move about a year ago. TCI has a great reputation," Maria responds. "But when I did my due diligence, I realized your company still has an arduous process for agents to submit applications to carriers. By my estimate, I would have had to work an additional two hours a day using your processes to submit the same number of policies. I just couldn't rationalize that."

Mike jumps in. "We've held out on making investments in new technology, but I can't believe that our processes are that time-consuming," he protests.

Maria reaches into her attaché case and pulls out her laptop. She opens it and clicks an icon to call up an application interface. She explains that SCI uses a standard application for life insurance with twenty questions that can be submitted to several carriers for quick policy quotes. Through the interface, carriers submitting quotes can request additional information—typically answers to four or five additional questions from prospective customers—so they can promptly provide more detailed quotes at preferred rates.

"That's amazing," Mike says. "How long has your firm had this tool?"

"About eighteen months."

Still staring at the screen of Maria's laptop, Mike asks, "Did your firm develop this interface on its own? How long did it take to work out the interface with all the carriers? And what kind of productivity gains have you seen? I've got a lot more questions, but this looks like a big win for SCI."

"Mike, I knew you were going to have a lot of questions, so I talked to our head of technology, Anthony Grout. Here's his business card. He loves to talk about this solution, and since we don't compete head to head with Tri Counties, Anthony will be happy to talk to you."

Nikki and Mike thank Maria for her time, finish off their coffee, and head for the car. "Where to next?" Mike asks.

"We're heading across town to talk to Tim Gerard," Nikki says.

"Come on, Nikki," Mike groans. "Tim is my poorest producing agent. How could spending time with him possibly help me figure out how to increase sales?"

"Remember, Mike, you're in my capable hands for the entire day. And after talking to Tim, we'll swing by the accounting department and talk with the team there," Nikki says. "By the end of today, you will have spoken with a top-producing agent and an agent who struggles to meet sales goals, and you'll have had an in-depth look at the numbers. If you're up for this, say, 'Ready.'"

"Ready," he responds, but with obviously tepid enthusiasm.

As they head back to the conference room after completing the first round of field assignments, Mike admits to himself that it has been an eye-opening day. They enter the room to see Sean and Phil with coffee cups in hand, as Sean shares the details of his son's progress on the Little League field. He looks up and asks, "So, Nikki, how did the interviews go?"

"Let's ask Mike," Nikki says.

"Well, we covered a lot a ground, literally," Mike says, settling in at the conference table. "I met the top agent from another firm and one of my agents who is having a hard time. And then we went over to the administrative office, where I met with folks from accounting, claims, and application processing. We even reviewed feedback from new clients through social media, surveys, and complaint calls."

"That's quite a round-up," Phil observes. "What did you take away from all that?"

Sean moves to the whiteboard to jot notes as Mike thinks through everything he has learned and decides to begin with the conversation with Maria. "I think there were probably two big takeaways there," he says. "The first is the passion she has for the business. It's infectious. I couldn't help but think that if we hired more agents with that kind of enthusiasm, half the battle would be won."

"How many agents work for you, Mike?" Phil asks.

"Eleven at the moment, and I would say that maybe only a third of them are passionate about their work."

"And why do you think that might be?" Phil asks gently.

"I've been rethinking that since my conversations today," Mike responds. "Part of it may be their workloads and the way they have to spend their time. At SCI, the agents use a new proprietary app. Maria says she can efficiently file 60, sometimes up to 75, applications monthly, whereas our busiest agents can only file 45 to 50. The bottom line is that her firm is using technology to increase the capacity of their sales agents so they can spend more time meeting with clients and less time processing applications."

As Sean writes notes, he asks, "What's the deal with this new app?"

"At Maria's invitation, I called SCI's head of technology on our way back here," Mike says. "It would be a big investment for us to implement the same kind of app here, but Anthony says they're open to a licensing arrangement. And there's more to come in the near future, like custom alerts to policyholders and special discounts, that kind of thing. If we're open to it, our technology team should talk with him."

Nikki jumps in. "I've known Maria for several years. She's a superstar agent. If we had the same technology, I know she'd come to work for TCI because our culture better suits her life goals. The implications for recruiting talented agents could be awesome."

"We'll come back to that," Sean says as he motions to Mike. "Keep the download coming."

"Next we visited Tim Gerard. He's one of the agents in my region," Mike explains for Phil's benefit. "He's been with us for a year. He is our team's lowest producing agent, but at the same time, he probably connects with our clients the best.

"It was interesting. I opened the dialogue by saying that our meeting wasn't a performance evaluation, but an assignment given to me by

Mr. McKinnon to help lead the team better. I told him Nikki was there as a mentor. We could see the tension in Tim's shoulders drop and his face brighten when he realized that he was being asked to help."

Mike summarizes Tim's perspectives on the challenges agents face in being productive and meeting their sales goals. Each carrier has a diverse range of policies and special requirements for submitting applications. Tim and his fellow agents spend a lot of time wading through the paperwork and keeping up with policy and price changes so they can help their clients secure the best coverage and right price.

"You know, I see his point," he adds. "The more analytical our carriers get with actuarial insights, the more complex and granular the application data becomes. For veteran agents, new policy requirements are fairly easy to absorb in terms of incremental learning, but for our new agents, it's a real mountain of knowledge to climb. I'm not sure what to do with this information, but it is a real problem if the only agents who can thrive are grizzled veterans. That limits our ability to recruit new agents and capitalize on their enthusiasm."

"How many applications does Tim submit per month?" Phil asks.

"Probably 20 to 25 per month." Mike pauses, considering what else to share with the team. "And then, we spoke to the 'Peace Keepers.'"

"The peace keepers?" Phil asks in confusion.

"That's our nickname for the operations team," Sean explains. "They handle application approval, premium collections, claims, and policy cancellations. They have to be peace keepers when juggling the demands of agents, clients, management, auditors, and more than 250 insurance carriers covering property and casualty, life and disability, annuities, and on and on."

Like others on the sales team, Mike has huge respect for the operations team and their professionalism, wealth of knowledge, and dedication to TCI. What he had not realized until their conversation today was how much they know about sales. The operations staff speaks with his sales agents more often than Mike does. They know which agents are struggling with paperwork and underwriting requirements, which ones have a hard time handling objections from clients, who's going to have a great month, and whose pipeline of applications is fragile or subject to high cancellations.

"The operations team is like an early warning system for a whole gambit of issues that I can help with, if I can find a way to tap into this live stream of real-time knowledge," Mike says. "How could I have missed that?"

He pauses, searching his brain for another detail from his conversation with operations that he wanted to share. Before he can remember it, he looks up and sees grins on the faces of Sean, Phil, and Nikki. What now?

"We have a gift for you, Mike," Phil says. Nikki slides a package across the table. It appears to be a book wrapped in brown paper, the way he used to make book covers for his school textbooks to protect them.

Mike opens the book, but it's empty. He looks up at them in confusion.

"It's a journal," Phil says. "Read the inscription on the inside front cover page of the journal."

"'Show me, don't tell me,'" Mike reads aloud and then pauses. "I don't get it."

Sean provides the explanation. "Keeping a journal can be a great way to capture good ideas so that you don't miss anything, so you can harvest the learning to improve professionally, to lead your team to greater success, and even to pursue your personal goals. Why leave something so important to the chance that you'll remember ideas that come at you out of the blue? You can use your journal to jot down your thoughts and input from other people and sources."

Sean notes that several people at TCI have adopted journaling as an everyday business practice. Some write in paper journals, and others keep a running journal on their laptop or tablet. As he explains that everyone has a different approach—some jot written notes, while others diagram or draw pictures of their ideas—Mike notes that Phil is writing in a black leather journal, and he recalls Nikki writing on her iPad as he was chatting with the operations team this morning. And his mind conjures the familiar sight of Sean sitting at his desk writing and drawing in a book regularly at the end of the work day, with a "Please do not disturb" sign on his door. Sean calls his end-of-day routine "cave time," and Mike had always assumed he was just going over his schedule for the next day on his desk calendar.

Mike flips through the blank pages of the journal, thinking about what his first entry might be. "I'll give it a try, and thank you, all of you," he says, looking at each of the people gathered around the conference table. "I've got a lot to think through, and writing it out may help me do that."

"OK," Sean says as he moves to the other whiteboard with the Learning Loop diagram. "Let's get back on track with a summary of today's field interviews. "

He writes "Assessing Performance" next to the "What is going on?" box in the loop diagram (see Figure 4.1). "To determine what is going on, leaders need to assess, not evaluate," Sean says. "That may seem like some kind of silly word play, but it's crucial to the process that we talk about the differences between assessing and evaluating. Assessing is an attempt to see what is happening without affixing value, good or bad, right or wrong. The more viewing points that a leader can harvest, the more likely we are to see things accurately and develop a more complete picture."

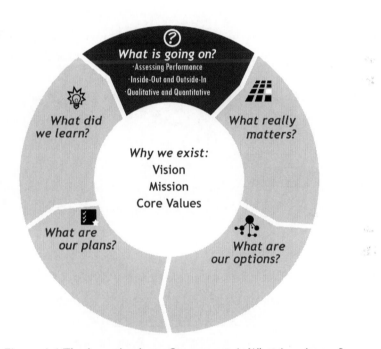

Figure 4.1 The Learning Loop Component 1: What is going on?

Some organizations conduct formal SWOT analyses to study strengths, weaknesses, opportunities, and threats, Sean notes, and others do environmental scans and organize focus groups, which are all forms of assessment. He looks first at Mike, and then at Nikki and Phil. Everyone nods their understanding, so he continues by putting two more entries on the whiteboard.

- Inside-Out and Outside-In

- Qualitative and Quantitative

"Mike, how might these apply to your field visits?" Sean asks.

"Well … we started by speaking with Maria, which I guess would be an example of Outside-In," Mike says. "She told us how the new technology her company uses allows agents to submit 60 to 75 applications a month, which offers quantitative information about the impact of the way they do business."

Phil asks, "If you hadn't spoken with Maria or anyone outside of TCI, do you think your insights from the day would be different?"

"I wouldn't have the information about technology that might, or might not, be useful to our firm," Mike says. "I might have gone on assuming that other companies go about their business pretty much the same way we do. But now I know that's not the case. And even if we don't adopt the same kind of technology solution, we know now that other agencies are working hard to improve their clients' experiences."

"Exactly," Sean says.

Nikki adds, "I appreciate that you are not making a judgment at this point about whether TCI should adopt this new technology. That's consistent with the protocol set out in the Learning Loop."

Next, Phil asks if Mike can supply an example of Inside-Out with a qualitative bent. Mike responds that in his conversations with the Peace Keepers, the operations staff didn't supply reports about turn times and application completion rates. Instead, they shared their views and possible conclusions based on their daily interactions with sales agents.

"When the ops team was describing their perspectives on how the agents are doing, what was running through your mind?" Phil asks.

"I was thinking that we could prove out their perceptions about each agent's performance by pulling reports and using quantitative data to test their qualitative observations," Mike says.

Sean jumps in, eager to make a point by sketching a 2 x 2 grid next to the Learning Loop (see Figure 4.2). "So a good tactic in assessing what is going on is to set up a matrix to catalog the possibilities of where—that's Outside-In and Inside-Out—we might assess and how—that's the Qualitative and Quantitative data—to garner the best vantage point of what's going on. This is a big issue, so we're applying a big level of effort. But our aim is always to establish a 360-degree view. In other words, we want to take a holistic approach."

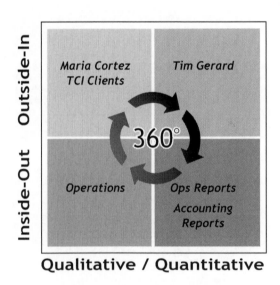

Figure 4.2 Viewing Points Matrix

Sean steps back and says, "Whew! I think we've accomplished a lot on our first day. What do you think?" Mike nods, still taking in the diagrams on the board and applying the ideas there to what he learned in his field conversations.

"I gotta say," he responds slowly, "I had no idea where this day was going when I walked through the door this morning. This is a lot to take in, but I'm already starting to feel like there are some answers out there."

"Great!" Sean says. "Let's pick this up in the morning then. Tomorrow, you'll talk with Phil about the next component of the Learning Loop, answering the question, What Really Matters?"

As Sean, Nikki, and Phil head out the door, they leave Mike seated at the table where he is busy jotting notes and sketching the diagrams from the whiteboard into his new journal, making his own notes as he goes.

Summary of Key Concepts

- **Assessing Performance.** Assessing is the process of seeing what is going on without affixing value, good or bad, right or wrong, and without applying personal biases. The more viewing points that leaders can gather, the greater their ability to understand an issue. The aim of leadership is to see things the way they really are. The more consequential the issue, the more thoughtful a leader needs to be when constructing a 360-degree view. Developing a simple matrix or a more complex inventory technique (e.g., SWOT analysis) helps ensure that the right level of effort is invested.

- **Outside-In and Inside-Out.** Viewing points from inside and outside the organization can help leaders garner a more multidimensional view of an issue. This holistic approach, which sometimes takes the form of a SWOT analyses or environmental scan, aims to reveal what may have previously gone unnoticed or been misunderstood.

- **Qualitative and Quantitative.** Information comes in varying forms, and some data are more subtle than others. Greater diversity of information enables more useful insights. Data from information systems is certainly an important source, but leaders often under-value qualitative data, which can be captured through field interviews. Humans have an uncanny way of imparting information with subtle meaning, which facilitates identifying and solving problems.

- **Level of Effort.** Sophisticated leaders are curious and capture information on a continuous basis through habits (e.g., journaling) and effective processes (e.g., "cave time" used for reflection and dialogue with mentors). These habits and processes can take years to develop, and executives who master them should be willing to share these productive habits with others.

Chapter 5

What Really Matters?

As Mike enters the conference room, he finds Phil already at work, peering intently at the screen of a laptop. Before Mike can even sit down next to him, Phil says enthusiastically, "I love this sales reporting system!

"I used to be the only one at the table for our quarterly meetings looking at paper reports. And then Jim gave me a laptop, and Sean spent some time showing me how to use the sales database. It's fantastic—so many ways to look at the numbers!"

Phil continues, "Your comment yesterday about validating the qualitative input from the operations team with quantitative data got me to thinking, so I've been looking at your sales team performance based on some of the issues the operations team mentioned, like the rate of applications converted to active policies."

Mike looks at the screen up on Phil's computer, a roster of his team's performance for last month (see Figure 5.1).

Agent Number	Applications Submitted	Applications Approved	Applications Delivered	Close Ratio
101	55	45	40	73%
102	45	40	38	84%
103	70	40	35	50%
104	55	40	38	69%
105*	42	27	18	43%

Figure 5.1 TCI Sales Report
* Agents with tenure of less than six months

"What do you do see, Mike?"

"Hmmm, I generally don't review these reports," Mike says, studying the numbers. "Well, first off, Tim, the new agent I spoke with yesterday, is agent 105. His low close ratio is disappointing, but not really a surprise. But the range of the other agents, from 84 percent to 50 percent, does take me aback. I need to figure out what might account for that."

"That struck me, too," Phil says, "so I've been running some numbers to look for possible correlations." He clicks through a series of tables and charts. One shows new insurance policies by agents based on tenure; after the first year, there seems to be no connection between years on the job and performance. Another shows the rate of applications to new policies based on customer demographics, such as age range and family status; again, no trends emerge. In fact, the only clear correlation is in the aging of the application: The longer it takes to approve the application, the less likely customers are to enroll.

Phil clicks to another screen, which shows the results of a recent TCI focus group study. At the top of the list of reasons for dissatisfaction is the statement: "Application process takes too long."

Mike sits back in his chair and closes his eyes for a moment. "I know all this data is out there, but I've only been focusing on results—premiums sold," he says slowly. "This data is really useful. The agents can't sell if we can't deliver on customers' expectations. If we could speed up the application process, that should translate into happier customers and more sales. More sales motivates agents, and motivated agents produce even more sales."

He pauses and then says, "I've been harping at my agents about improving their sales skills when maybe I should have been talking with Ops about possible solutions to speed up the application process. At the very least, we should be reviewing the application aging report together on a regular basis."

"In other words," Phil says, "sales could increase if you keep your focus on what really matters." He points to the sheet of paper on the table left there from their first meeting with the vision statement: We exist to help our policyholders thrive—however they define it.

Phil moves to the whiteboard and jots the words "Customer orientation" next to the What really matters? component of the Learning Loop (Figure 5.2). "A lot of companies talk about customer orientation, but TCI's vision statement puts it at the center of what we do," he notes. "And you're right about that positive spiral: Everything we do with the customer in mind will likely increase sales."

Figure 5.2 The Learning Loop Component 2: What really matters?

Phil turns back to the whiteboard and writes "Stakeholders' needs" as he says, "Of course, our policyholders aren't the only people we need to think about in considering what really matters. What about the people who help TCI deliver on its vision and mission? If it matters to our stakeholders, it matters to the company. We've already talked about you partnering more effectively with Operations and your sales agents. Can you think of other stakeholders that you should be accounting for?"

"Well, you, Mr. McKinnon, and the other owners," Mike responds. "If anybody has a stake in TCI, it's you."

Phil nods in approval and motions with his hand: Keep going.

"We rely on our insurance carriers, so maybe I should reach out to some of them to see how we might work together to improve our service?"

Again Phil nods and gestures to keep the ideas coming, but Mike is stumped.

"How about Finance and Accounting?" Phil asks. "They're not just the people you talk to about the annual budget or the need to approve variances. As a leader in this organization, you need to understand your team's contribution to the financial well-being of the mission of this company—how you help to fuel TCI's economic engine. Do you know the impact to net income if your team doesn't meet sales projections? Who can you ask about the financial implications of any possible solutions or improvements you might identify?"

Mike nods, but Phil is already gesturing for him to identify additional stakeholders.

"Oh, come on, Phil!" Mike says in exasperation.

"All right, I'll help you with this one. It may not be obvious," Phil says. "What about Megan, Jake, and Jessica?"

That suggestion surprises Mike, and he takes a moment to answer. "My family is my top priority, but we're talking about solving work issues here," he says slowly. "I've always prided myself on my ability to keep family and work separate. I compartmentalize."

"But are they really separate?" Phil counters. "Isn't your family one of the reasons you're here—to provide for them? And to set an example for your kids of working hard to succeed? We all face the challenge of prioritizing what matters to us most. Have you ever noticed that Nikki leaves here every day at 5:30 sharp?"

"Sure."

"She heads over to her mother's house in Fallbrook to fix her dinner and help her to bed, so she doesn't have to move to an assisted living facility," Phil says softly. "I asked Nikki if I could share that story because I think it's very instructive about how to honor family while advancing one's career."

Phil continues, "The point is that as you develop your action plan, it's important to consider all the stakeholders—and that includes you and your family. Will you do that?"

Mike thinks about how his work days have gotten longer and longer in recent months and how his worries about work have nagged at his attention even when he is with his family. He sees the potential to steer things in a better direction—for his sales team, for the people he loves, and for himself—and he acknowledges this opportunity as a gift. "Yes, sir, I can do that," he says.

Mike takes a walk after his long session with Phil and decides to stop for lunch at his favorite diner. When he walks in, the first people he sees are Steve, one of the operations managers he spoke to yesterday, and Amy, a financial analyst Mike has met briefly once or twice. Mike hesitates at the door, thinking he would rather avoid seeing someone from TCI, but Steve is already waving him over to pull up a seat at their table.

Lunch turns out to be quite pleasant. Steve and Amy are not just colleagues, but a couple as well. They chat about their favorite lunch spots and then about Steve's passion for cooking. "Dating an amateur chef is a gift from heaven," Amy says with a laugh, "because I love good food—but I hate spending time in the kitchen."

On the walk back to the office, the conversation turns back to TCI, when Steve asks how Mike's research is going. "Making good progress, but I may be back in your office soon with more questions," Mike says. He mentions the need to review application aging statistics more frequently and to discuss ideas for speeding up the application process.

"We've been talking over the same issues in Ops and with other sales managers," Steve acknowledges. "It would be good to get together in the same room, look at the numbers, and start identifying solutions."

"And I'd like to talk to you and your colleagues in Finance, too," Mike says, turning to Amy. "Could you help me quantify how my sales team contributes to TCI's bottom line? It might be helpful to understand the specifics."

"Oh, sure," Amy responds. "I think we can provide some really useful data about short-term and long-term revenue production from the types of policies your agents are selling. We like to say that some blocs of business provide higher octane fuel than others to power TCI's economic engine."

Mike smiles. "That's the second time today I've heard the phrase *economic engine*."

When Phil and Sean enter the conference room after lunch, they find Mike at the whiteboard. He has added the words "Economic engine" to the list next to What really matters? and is studying the diagram.

Sean laughs. "And so the student becomes the teacher."

Mike grins back. "Just making my small contribution to the work at hand. I had lunch with specialists from Operations and Finance today, and they shared some good ideas about the next steps I could take in exploring how best to get my sales team back on track."

Mike turns back to the table and the notes he has made in his journal from the day's conversations. He shares some of the questions he has formulated based on the reports he reviewed with Phil and on Steve and Amy's suggestions.

"I think I've just been spinning my wheels focusing on the declining sales numbers without looking for other data that might help identify possible solutions," Mike says. "I really need to expand the repertoire of business analytics that may be relevant to sales and review those forecasts and reports on a regular basis."

Sean and Phil look over Mike's questions and the next steps he has identified to continue to gather useful data, and they add a few ideas of their own. After agreeing to convene again the following morning, Mike heads back to his office to catch up on his work and check on and respond to messages and email.

As Mike pulls into his driveway after work, he is startled to realize that his headlights are not illuminating the house. For the second night in a row, he is home before dark, in time for supper with Megan and the kids. It feels good.

His wife apparently feels the same way. "Let's make this a habit," she says with a laugh as she takes a break from dinner preparations to give him a quick hug. "Why don't you take over helping Jessica practice her spelling words while I finish up here?"

"Daddy, Daddy, I got a new Horton book from the library today so we can read that tonight!" Jake announces as he runs in to greet his father.

"Great, buddy!" Mike says. He hugs both the kids, takes the spelling list, and begins calling off words for his daughter to spell.

After dinner, the family clears the table together, and Jake begins calling off words for his sister to spell: "Plate!" "Spoon!" "Glass!" Mike chimes in, "Spaghetti Bolognese!" Jessica laughs and protests, "Dad, those are not second-grade words!"

Mike looks fondly at his wife and children. "My favorite stakeholders," he says.

"Huh?" Jake says, looking up at his father.

"Never mind, buddy. Now where's that new Horton book?"

After tucking in the kids, Mike and Megan collapse on the couch. "So," Megan says nonchalantly, "work is going better?"

Mike had been too tired the previous night to share with his wife what was happening at the office. Tonight, though, he eagerly tells her about the last couple days—his meeting with Mr. McKinnon, his initial concerns about the "intervention," the concept of the Learning Loop, and everything he has learned in his conversations with Sean, Phil, and Nikki and from his field assignments.

"I've got a lot to do, and I'm still not sure whether and how this will translate to increased sales, but I feel … hopeful," he concludes.

"That's a good thing," Megan says. "And I'm glad you work at a place where the bosses respond to setbacks in such a positive way—not blaming and threatening."

She thinks for a moment and then adds, "You know, that Learning Loop is interesting. It feels like something we could use in setting our own goals for ourselves and our family."

"You may be right," Mike says, and then he yawns. "But not tonight, OK, honey?"

Summary of Key Concepts

- **Customer Orientation.** The first check on what matters most to an organization aiming to achieve its full potential is to identify the issues that matter most to its customers. Addressing those issues is the purpose of the enterprise, the reason it exists. A customer-focused, mission-driven enterprise can tap into an intrinsic wellspring of motivation and energy when its plans are aligned with its mission. If it matters to its customers, it matters to the enterprise. The enterprise may not be able to solve every issue for its customers but should strive to understand—in rank order, if possible—what customers need and want.

- **Stakeholders' Needs.** Stakeholders are persons or groups that help an enterprise execute on its mission: employees, vendors, strategic partners, and constituents in the communities where it resides. Achieving the full potential of the enterprise hinges on how well it understands the needs of stakeholders and, maybe more importantly, acts on them. If it matters to stakeholders, it matters to the enterprise.

- **Economic Engines.** Leaders across the enterprise need a working knowledge of which activities generate the revenue that sustains it. Leaders should understand how their department or division contributes to the economic well-being of the enterprise. To achieve a sufficient understanding of what powers the economic engine of the enterprise, leaders must develop granular views and revisit those views at intervals that facilitate timely interventions and forecasts that enable growth or abandonment.

Chapter 6

What Are Our Options?

Mike heads directly into the conference room the next morning, expecting to find Sean, Phil, and Nikki. But instead Sammy Tanaka, the businessman with an office down the hall from Mike, sits at the table alone.

"Uh, good morning, Sammy," Mike says uncertainly.

"Hello, Mike, it's good to see you." Sammy rises and extends his hand. "I know you didn't expect to see me here, but Sean thought it might be a good idea if I introduced you to the third component of my Learning Loop."

"Your .... Learning Loop?"

"Indeed." Sammy slides a photocopied article from a business journal across the table, and Mike sees the title, "The Learning Loop: A

Framework for Business Organizations to Thrive by Fostering Innovation and Continual Growth." The author's name is Osamu Tanaka.

"As you can see from the date, I wrote this article several years ago," Sammy says. "Jim liked the Learning Loop model so much he adopted it for use here at TCI." He pauses and then continues. "May I share with you the story of how the Learning Loop came to be?"

"Of course," Mike says, turning his attention away from the article before him. "I'd be honored to hear it."

Osamu Tanaka was one of Jim McKinnon's most successful sales agents in the early days of Tri Counties Insurance. "Sammy" joined the firm after meeting Jim when he helped the Tanaka family through a rough spot in its import-export business: A warehouse fire had caused extensive damage, but because the business had adequate insurance coverage through TCI, it was able to carry on.

A decade after joining TCI, Sammy resigned from the company to look after his ailing grandfather. The Tanaka family had reviewed all their options for caring for their patriarch and ultimately agreed that Sammy's offer to relocate to Japan would be the best solution. Looking back on his grandfather's final months, Sammy was glad he had the honor to spend time with him. He learned a great deal about his family's history and native culture. In turn, his grandfather was fascinated to learn about the Tanaka family business in America and introduced Sammy to several valuable contacts.

After his grandfather's death, Sammy remained in Japan for several years, reopening an office for the Tanaka business there. Tanaka International had opened a Japanese office several years previously, but sales quickly skyrocketed beyond the division's ability to fulfill orders. Rather than risk the ire of long-time customers, the company closed the Japanese office and focused on building its business from the San Diego base. Under his father's guidance and using what he had learned from his years with TCI, Sammy plotted an ambitious but realistic course for the new office and hired knowledgeable, experienced staff to help it thrive.

In fact, the Japanese office did so well that the family decided to open a third office in Vancouver, British Columbia, and Sammy volunteered to head those new operations. He began to codify what he had found to be successful in launching new initiatives, tracking their progress, and correcting course when necessary. He eventually wrote the article on the table before Mike and submitted it for publication. When Tanaka International reorganized upon his father's retirement, Sammy decided to pursue a new direction. He opened Tanaka Enterprise, a consulting firm based in the office leased from TCI. Sammy now travels widely to meet with businesses across the United States and Canada on how to apply the Learning Loop to their operations.

As Sammy pauses at the end of his story, Mike takes the opportunity to say, "I had no idea a business guru was just down the hall from me."

Sammy laughs. "No one has ever called me that before. I prefer the title Fellow Learner."

"I can see why Sean thought you'd be a great person to help me understand the Learning Loop," Mike says.

"From what Sean and Phil have told me, you've taken to this approach with an open mind and enthusiasm, and I know from our past conversations that you have a great mind for business and a dedication to this company," Sammy responds. "I've shared my own story with you this morning because I think it may help to illustrate some of the key points in the next stage of the Learning Loop, identifying options."

As Sammy rises and moves to the whiteboard, Mike notices that the third component of the loop has been filled in with the question, What are our options? (see Figure 6.1). Below that question are three points:

- The Magic of Options

- Our Full Potential

- Fair Exchange of Values

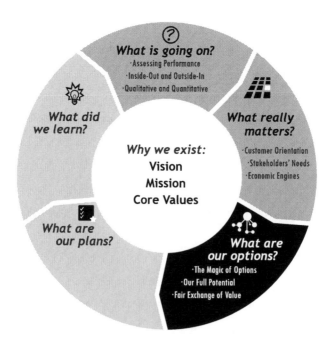

Figure 6.1 The Learning Loop Component 3: What are our options?

Pointing to the first entry, Sammy notes that people often applaud "quick thinking" although this is not always the best approach to solving business problems. Especially complex issues, like declining sales, may result from a variety of causes, such as economic shifts, new entrants in the market, and changes in consumers' preferences and expectations. A willingness to explore all the possible causes and solutions and to invite and consider the perspectives of many stakeholders drives curiosity and creativity, which may generate even more options.

A common misstep in business organizations is for a leader to champion a single idea, Sammy continues. It might be the first idea that comes to mind, or an idea that is easy to implement or clearly superior to another readily apparent option. These snap judgments may shut down prematurely the creative and collaborative exploration of a wider range of ideas, from all ranks and departments of the business and from outside—from the competition and other business sectors or industries. In other words, quick decisions may short-circuit creative problem solving.

When leaders remain open to considering many options, the best outcomes are more likely to emerge. Some companies turn to consultants and outside "experts" for guidance when they might be better off relying on their collective knowledge of their business, combined with environmental scans of their competition and market, to identify the best options among the possible solutions they puzzle out. Instead of paying lots of money for answers they already know, successful leaders trust their instincts and those of their staff.

On the other hand, Sammy notes, working with consultants can be extremely useful in helping an organization identify and vet options to address novel problems or solutions. "And I'm not just saying that because that's what I do," he adds with a smile.

"So, Mike, based on everything you've learned so far in your field interviews and diving into the data, what ideas to improve performance are emerging?" Sammy asks.

"Well," Mike says slowly, "I think one option might be to improve the connections between our sales and operations teams. They see the business from differing perspectives, and if they had the opportunity to work together and share ideas, I think a lot of good could come from that."

Mike explains that he's thinking about proposing a regular meeting with his agents and a revolving group of operations and finance specialists, maybe every other Monday morning initially. Mondays might work best for sales because it's a down day for agents: They bring in most of their applications and signed policies later in the week and on Saturdays; Mike has noticed a strong pattern in the sales data that clients aren't inclined to schedule appointments on Mondays.

"The processors know all the fine points about the products from our wide range of insurance carriers, so they can transfer that knowledge to the agents," he notes. "And this kind of meeting would be a good place to study the pipeline reports as well—to review the status of applications and rates of closing new policies."

"What else?" Sammy asks.

"We need to consider our options for improving the customer experience and streamlining the application process, which takes too long right now," Mike responds. "We could talk to SCI about licensing their app. Our company doesn't want to become a tech developer, but their solution might help us to get up to speed quickly and, hopefully, cost-effectively."

Mike continues, even picking up speed. "And I think we need to revisit our new employee training and re-evaluate the level of support we provide for new agents in the first ninety days. That's a critical period," he says. "But I've noticed that some of the veteran agents are lagging, so I may need to meet with them outside of our annual performance review to talk things through."

"Those are all great ideas, but you may need to think about setting some priorities about the order in which you implement them," Sammy says.

He gestures toward the second component under What are our options? "Our Full Potential." "An enterprise can have brilliant ideas, but without careful planning to implement them, it may fail to realize its full potential," he notes.

TCI needs to chart its optimal trajectory, somewhere between such a steep path of implementation that the company ends up in distress and such a shallow curve that it drifts toward complacency. Sammy suggests that good leaders do their part to help the organization chart a trajectory that is somewhere in the middle—stimulating stakeholders to grow personally and professionally. When every stakeholder is challenged and supported to contribute maximum effort, the enterprise moves forward at its own top speed and achieves its full potential for that operating period or cycle.

Sammy sketches a line chart depicting a growth curve on the whiteboard next to the Learning Loop (see Figure 6.2). The curve starts out with a slow rise that gets steeper over time. "The question is, how much tension can the organization withstand? You can't do everything at once," he cautions. "At the same time, you can drive it into the ground through sheer boredom if you're not continually on the lookout for opportunities to sync up with customers' needs and move forward."

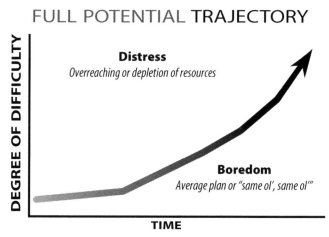

FULL POTENTIAL TRAJECTORY

Figure 6.2 Optimal Trajectory for Achieving Organizational Potential

Every organization must chart its own unique path and monitor its progress toward ambitious but doable goals that can be measured quantifiably through such benchmarks as net income and capital growth. Leaders must assess which options the organization can implement without overreaching or depleting its resources, while at the same time challenging people to move past the "same ol', same ol'" approach.

"Your growth curve is different from every other organization based on your goals, your mission, and your decisions on deploying resources," he adds. "Don't be disheartened if your growth isn't as fast as others, as long as it's moving at a rate that feels like the appropriate tension for your company."

"Well, the current rate of my sales team certainly doesn't feel right," Mike mutters. "But with these new options on the table, we should be able to pick up the pace. So, what's that third item on the list, Fair Exchange of Value?"

"It's about aiming for win/wins with all your stakeholders," Sammy replies. "Your customers need to see value in getting insurance coverage through TCI. Your sales agents need to feel that their efforts in building the business are appreciated, both in terms of monetary rewards and in recognition from the company's leaders. TCI needs to be fairly compensated by the carriers. Can you think of other examples of fair exchange of value, Mike?"

Mike thinks for a moment. "Well, I guess since Megan and the kids are stakeholders, they need to see the value for the family in my work." He hesitates. "And I'm not just talking about my paycheck. They need to see that my work for TCI is good for me—that when I go off to work every day, it's to take on challenges that I find interesting and fulfilling. I've never wanted to be one of those people who thinks of their work as the sacrifice they make to support themselves and their family."

"Very true," Sammy says. "I found the same dynamic at play when I worked for the family business. I enjoyed the niche I created for myself in launching new outlets for our company. And then when the time was right for me, I moved on to a new challenge."

Sammy and Mike talk through some of the tools TCI has to measure a sustainable exchange of value with its stakeholders: modeling, forecasting, scenario planning, and performance reviews that encourage employees to share their professional and personal goals for growth. Then Sammy suggests that the next step for Mike might be to apply the newest components of the Learning Loop to what he has learned so far and to consider possible next steps.

When Sean checks in with Mike an hour later, he is deeply intent on his planning, dividing his time between consulting sales reports on his laptop and making notes and sketches in his journal. Mike looks up at Sean with a smile. He shows Sean a short list in his journal, eager to share his ideas on prioritizing what appear to be the best options to increase sales:

1. Convene biweekly Monday meetings between the sales team and operations staff to review pipeline reports and share ideas.

2. Investigate options to streamline applications, including negotiating a licensing arrangement for the SCI app.

3. Upgrade training and support for new sales agents.

4. Schedule regular individual sessions with all sales agents to talk through how to help them achieve their full potential.

5. Analyze revenue streams with various carriers to ensure that TCI is receiving a fair exchange of value in its commissions.

"This is great—a really comprehensive list!" Sean says. "I've been thinking about the fifth one myself recently, especially since we've been talking about our economic engine. Where do we make money? We sell the policies our clients need, but are we being fairly compensated for providing that service? It's been a while since we reviewed our commission schedules."

Another way to ensure a fair exchange of value with the carriers is to improve operational efficiency, he notes. If some carriers are unwilling to change their commissions, they might be amenable to streamlining their application requirements and underwriting processes so that agents can generate more applications and close more policies in less time.

"You know," Sean adds thoughtfully, "we might want to talk to a few of our insurance carriers about the possibility of them subsidizing the licensing fees for that new application system. It could be a win/win for them, too."

He shifts to Mike's idea about meeting with sales agents. "When you and I get together for our quarterly lunches, our conversations about your personal goals and pursuits aren't just idle chitchat. I want to know what matters most to you personally as well as professionally," he says.

Mike thinks back to a meeting he had with Sean and Mr. McKinnon when he got his promotion to regional sales manager. At the end of that meeting, Mr. McKinnon invited him to keep in touch. "TCI's vision is to help our policyholders thrive—and one way to do that is to make sure our people thrive," he told Mike. "Successful leaders know how their employees define a better future and what their professional goals and personal dreams are."

Mike shares that recollection with Sean. "I realized at the time that Mr. McKinnon was reminding me about one of my new responsibilities—to get to know each member of my sales team and to relate to them personally," he says. "In the crush of everyday business, I guess that's kind of fallen by the wayside."

Sean nods in agreement. "My wife is a teacher, and she has this mantra about her students that I think also applies to managers and employees: 'They don't care what you know unless they know you care,'" he says. "I've found that relating to agents on a personal level and being supportive about their personal aspirations helps maintain motivation. They're more invested in TCI's success when they can see that the company is invested in theirs.

"I know that Taylor, your counterpart in the Orange County region, is working on her MBA, and Jen is not only the person who keeps this office running smoothly but also plays a mean piano with a local jazz quartet," he continues. "When I was leading a sales team, I made a point to know who was coaching their kids' ball team and who was house hunting. High-achieving employees put a lot of dedication into their work. Reflecting that dedication by demonstrating an interest in them conveys that you care about their goals and want to support them in achieving their full potential."

"And when our people achieve their full potential, so does TCI," Mike says. "I get that. It's something that I've always known and appreciated about this organization, but I think I've gotten away from my part in making that happen for my sales team. I think scheduling more regular interactions with each agent will help make that happen."

Mike quickly understands that this mantra has wide applicability in optimizing business interactions and in connecting with others. That dynamic is what allowed him to thrive in his early years with TCI—the knowledge that his bosses cared about his success, and not just because his sales numbers were so phenomenal. And through his conversations with them, his clients could sense that he cared about their needs. That was one of the attributes that made him such a good agent. It dawns on Mike that he learned that approach through his interactions with Sean and Mr. McKinnon, even if he had never put it into those words: I cared about what they could teach me because I knew they cared. I need to live that model for my agents, too, to help them thrive as I have.

Mike and Sean return to the list of options, talking through the priorities, identifying colleagues from across the organization who need to be involved in planning and implementation, and settling on a tentative timeline. They agree that the highest priority needs to be given to the options that will likely have the greatest impact on increasing sales while at the same time operationalizing TCI's mission.

"So, I'll see you back here tomorrow morning?" Sean asks.

"OK, but ... I've got a lot to do here already. I feel like we've made a lot of progress, and I want to keep the momentum going," Mike says.

"You have, and I appreciate what you're saying," Sean responds easily. "We just need to cover the last couple components of the Learning Loop to help you maintain that momentum. Over the next couple mornings, we'll close the loop. By the way, did you enjoy your conversation with Sammy?"

"It was fascinating—and useful. I have to admit I feel kind of sheepish that I didn't realize that Sammy is such a well-respected business consultant," Mike says. "So, what's up for tomorrow?"

"Tomorrow," Sean says, "we move from options to planning and implementation."

Summary of Key Concepts

- **The Magic of Options.** It is not unusual for leaders to champion an idea; however, they need to suspend anchoring on the "one right answer" until all options are weighed objectively. Careful consideration of several options creates a "magic" that drives curiosity, openness, and creativity, which in turn generates even more options. And the more options leadership creates, the better outcomes the enterprise will produce. Leaders should hold open planning processes to facilitate this magic.

- **Our Full Potential.** Every enterprise has several performance trajectories on its way to full potential. Too steep a trajectory places the enterprise in distress, while too shallow a path may cause the organization to drift toward complacency, even boredom. Somewhere in the middle lies a challenging trajectory that stimulates stakeholders to grow personally and professionally. When every stakeholder is challenged to contribute maximum effort, the enterprise moves forward at full speed and achieves its full potential for that moment in time or business cycle.

- **Fair Exchange of Value.** As leaders work though options for helping individuals and the enterprise reach their full potential, particular attention, modeling, forecasting, and scenario planning should be considered to demonstrate a sustainable fair exchange of value with stakeholders, often referred to as a win/win.

Chapter 7

What Are Our Plans?

Mike spends a busy afternoon on the phone with Anthony Grout talking through possibilities for licensing fees, terms, and implementation of the new app and lining up planning and implementation meetings with sales, operations, and finance managers.

The next morning, he heads into the conference room ready to talk details with Sean but stops in the doorway, surprised by the presence of the person standing at the whiteboard studying the Learning Loop diagram.

"Good morning, Mike," Mr. McKinnon says. "Sean's been sharing some of the great ideas you're looking into. I wanted to take the opportunity to reiterate my support and to say that I'll be intrigued to hear what this new technology might do for TCI."

Mr. McKinnon turns back to the whiteboard. "Seeing this loop reminded me of when Sammy introduced us to this framework. Looking back, I think it's not an exaggeration to say that implementing these principles helped save the company."

"Really?" Mike responds. "I've always had the impression that TCI worked like a well-oiled machine, chugging forward through good times and tough times."

Mr. McKinnon takes a seat at the table and motions for Mike to join him. "That has been the case over the last decade or so, but there was a point when we had to overhaul that machine to get it working right," he says. Almost as if he is thinking aloud, the CEO recalls how his original company, McKinnon Insurance, grew quickly, acquired two other firms, and became TCI.

"Business had been going great, with double-digit growth for five years running. We were developing the plans for this building as our new headquarters and opening new satellite offices when, *bam!*, it was like we hit a wall." A nationwide recession seemed to hit the local economy especially hard. Several large manufacturers shut down, driving up regional unemployment. Across the board, TCI's sales went flat and started to decline. A couple top agents went to work for competitors, further lowering morale.

"In our strategic planning that year, we came up with lots of great ideas," he recalls. "We decided to be bold and pursue them all. But by midyear, it was obvious we had overstepped. We'd launched this new sales training initiative, but it didn't seem to generate much in the way of results. Finance was warning that we were going to be running into some cash flow headaches, and everybody was close to burning out. Then, one day, Sammy stopped by to inquire about the possibility of leasing an office in our new HQ, which was under construction in the midst of all this mayhem. Sammy asked innocuously, 'How are things going?' And I guess I just let loose about ... everything."

At that point, Sammy offered his consulting services, and Mr. McKinnon convened a mid-year session of the company's owners and executive team to revisit the strategic plan and regroup. "We covered a lot of the same ground you have over the last few days," he tells Mike wryly. "We recognized the need to refocus on doing what really matters—doing right by our customers and staff as our top priority. That meant pulling back on some of our new initiatives and figuring out why we weren't getting the results we expected from that sales training."

"Aah, I remember those days," Sean says as he enters the room and conversation. "I have to admit, when Sammy introduced the Learning Loop, I was not impressed. I thought, 'Duh, we know all this already.' But then as we started to talk it through, I realized we hadn't been practicing it. I think we all had a collective 'eureka!' moment in those sessions."

Mr. McKinnon nods and asks Sean, "And when did that moment come?"

Sean thinks for a moment and says slowly, "I think it was at a point when we were discussing the sales training. Everybody was talking about what they thought it was supposed to accomplish, and all of our statements were close, but not exactly the same. The sales managers from different regions seemed to have different expectations from how Ops and Finance seemed to be saying we should measure results. And then Sammy just said, 'Show me, don't tell me.'" That stopped us all in our tracks, trying to figure out what he meant."

Sean moves to the Learning Loop diagram and writes "Show Me, Don't Tell Me" next to the loop's fourth component, What are our plans? (see Figure 7.1).

Figure 7.1 The Learning Loop Component 4: What are our plans?

At that point, Sean continues, Sammy suggested that TCI's top executives formulate a written plan about the aims of the sales training and relate that plan back to the company's mission and vision statements. He explained that doing the work of creating written plans would engage a different level of thinking than sharing ideas verbally. Committing those plans to written form would require executives to think more carefully about doing what matters and communicate their thinking more clearly. Once the executive team talked through and completed a written plan spelling out high-level strategy, managers could more productively come up with tactics to execute those strategies on a team, department, and enterprise level.

Mr. McKinnon chimes in, "By the time we completed that process, we'd come to realize that there was some confusion over our strategic goals. By committing everything to a written plan, we began speaking more consistently about our strategies. In effect, we settled on a common language, a lexicon."

"And over time, we found it helpful to develop some templates for operationalizing the tactics the team agreed on, which led to a more systemic process for implementation and execution—and eventually, testing and assessing whether we were staying on track," Sean says. "Out of that period of crisis, we put together a solid foundation that has served us well to this day."

"So what you're telling me is that the Learning Loop is not just some abstraction," Mike says.

"That's exactly right," Mr. McKinnon concurs. "And now I think I'll leave you and Sean to put it to work on your current challenge."

With a few more words of encouragement, Mr. McKinnon heads down the hall toward his office, leaving the two remaining men to look pensively over the list of options in Mike's journal. Sean stands and heads toward the whiteboard, where he diagrams a matrix with the word "Impact" down the side and "Mission" along the bottom.

"I find it helpful sometimes to sketch things out as a way to compare and organize how they all fit together," he says. "So if we want to prioritize the options you've identified, we can assess the level of impact they will have on the organization and whether each is highly aligned with the mission or less so. Then we pinpoint them on the matrix where that assignment of impact and mission intersects."

Sean explains one other element that can be rendered with the planning matrix—assigning a relative size for each option, based on the resources, both in manpower and financial costs, required to implement it. A larger circle conveys that several people and/or departments will need to work together to implement the option—and that it might carry a relatively higher price tag (see Figure 7.2).

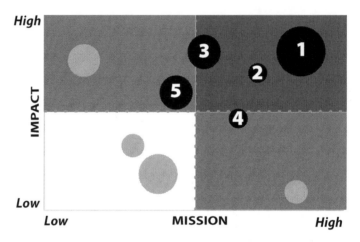

Figure 7.2 Prioritizing Matrix

They talk through the various aspects of the five options Mike has listed, agree on their relative impact and alignment to mission, and estimate the likely resources each will require. In the end, they agree that streamlining the application process will likely have the greatest impact for TCI's customers and staff but also require more resources. The biweekly meetings between sales and operations staff could also help boost sales and would be relatively inexpensive to implement. Along the same lines, the idea of Mike scheduling regular individual sessions with his agents is a small ticket item financially but is well aligned with the company's mission and has the potential to have a significant impact on sales.

The other two ideas fall a little farther away from the "sweet spot" of the matrix, they agree. Upgrading new agent training and analyzing revenue streams with carriers merit further study once they have implemented the top three ideas.

Mike sits back from the table. "Now we move from planning to action, right?"

"Yes. From ideas to implementation," Sean says as he moves to the whiteboard. Below the fourth component of the Learning Loop, What Are Our Plans?, he writes "Show Me, Don't Tell Me" and then "Aims, Goals, Strategies, Tactics, and Outcomes."

"Earlier in our conversation with Jim, I mentioned the templates we'd developed to operationalize the strategies the executive team agrees on," Sean continues. He reaches for a folder he had brought with him into the room and pulls out a document that he slides across the table to Mike. It's the result of the strategic planning process earlier in the year.

"I know this is familiar because you're listed alongside a couple of the projects," Sean says. "We'd like you to take the lead on developing the priorities we've identified this morning, and using this template should facilitate that process."

The next step will be to chunk down the big ideas into more granular and actionable components of initiatives, projects, and tasks, he explains. From that point, it will be easier to organize the work to be done by establishing roles and responsibilities, reporting requirements, due dates, and resources to deliver the desired project outcomes.

As Mike develops this and future initiatives, Sean recommends that he follow this progression from ideas to implementable steps:

1. Find your purpose.

2. Translate your purpose into S.M.A.R.T. goals that are specific, measurable, attainable, relevant, and timely.

3. Identify the key strategies that will help you achieve your goals.

4. Ensure that goals and strategies align with the organization's mission, vision, and values.

5. Develop tactics to put your strategies into action.

6. Spell out the outcomes you plan to achieve.

Mike nods as Sean enumerates the steps of the planning process. This is more familiar ground, as the strategic planning teams he has been involved with began their planning with an overview of the process.

"I will admit that I have a hard time occasionally differentiating between strategies and tactics," Mike says.

Sean offers an example to help clarify. "Let's say a guy who is nearing the half-century mark—not naming names or anything," he says, with a smile that lets Mike know this will be a personal story, "decides he wants to be more vibrant and active. That is his purpose. To achieve his purpose, he realizes that his goal must be to get healthier by losing 25 pounds over the next six months. That goal is specific and measurable. It's also attainable and definitely relevant to his purpose, and he assigns a timeframe as well."

Sean continues. "Next he identifies the strategies of eating healthier and becoming more active. He knows he'll have to integrate those strategies into his lifestyle going forward to stay true to his purpose. Then he turns to tactics. He and his wife start planning a menu for healthier dinners, and he alternates lunching at a nearby restaurant with low-cal options with bringing lunches that consist of salads and lean meat. He also settles on the tactic of getting up early three days a week to take a run before going to work.

"The difference between strategies and tactics is that strategies are higher level and less likely to change until the goal is achieved, whereas tactics are more flexible," he adds. "If the guy in this example decides that the morning run isn't working out for him, he can scrap it and try something else or supplement his runs with more exercise throughout the week."

Unlike the man in this example, Sean notes, Mike will need to share his implementation plan with a wider group, so the planning template should guide him ultimately to develop a one-page document to communicate with the teams he will be convening. But initially in the planning process, Sean advises Mike to identify and reach out to key stakeholders and convene a group dialogue to formulate purpose, goals, strategies, and tactics. In the bargain, being inclusive should enhance clarity and calibration of each stakeholder's grasp of the work ahead, facilitate the iteration of strategies and tactics, and increase buy-in.

"This is a lot to take in, I know," Sean says. "Are you ready to get started with this planning?"

"Ready," Mike says. "I've been taking notes about who to contact first."

"Great," Sean responds, "but before you dig in, we have one more aspect to cover under this component of the Learning Loop." He returns to the whiteboard and writes "Accountability & Clarity." Under that entry, he adds five numbers: 365, 252, 90, 30, and 1.

The planning document provides a framework for identifying what must be done, by whom, and when, Sean notes, and it addresses outcomes as well so that its champions can assess in a concrete way whether the initiative is achieving its intended purpose.

"Teamwork is most effective when there's a captain at the helm," he notes. "Leaders must know when to inspect and validate whether their teams are on course—and do so on intervals that facilitate timely course correction, if necessary. As the champion of the new application process, for example, you'll need to identify the causal link between activities your team is undertaking and the results you aim to produce. And you'll need to take steps to ensure that everyone on the team understands their charge and shares ownership of and accountability for the project."

Sean points to the final section of the planning document, which specifies short-term and long-term outcomes. Mike will need to identify which qualitative and quantitative measures will be used to assess whether the initiative is on track and what results it is generating. Some of those measures may be monitored daily (365) or every business day (252), some monthly (30), some quarterly (90), and some annually (1).

For example, the percentage of TCI clients using the new app as a self-service channel might be monitored on a daily basis for at least the first year after its launch, while the application-to-policy ratio of individual agents might be assessed daily, weekly, or biweekly. The company might commit to monthly client satisfaction surveys, especially in that first year after introducing the app, to assess its impact closely, and it might convene client and agent focus groups every three months.

"There's so much data out there, it can be dizzying if you try to collect and monitor it all on a frequent basis, so you have to choose carefully which data will likely provide the clearest assessment and how often you need to examine it," Sean adds. "You might want to monitor your agents' sales ratios on a daily or weekly basis, so you can step in immediately and provide support if you see a downward trend—and encourage and congratulate them when they're doing well. But with the focus groups, quarterly meetings are probably frequent enough to give agents and clients some time to use the app and note what works and doesn't work for them."

"This all makes sense, but I've got to admit, I never thought about how much work goes into producing these planning documents," Mike says. "Guess I'd better get going."

"It is a lot of work," Sean agrees, "but it pays off over the long term. Taking the time up-front to identify the purpose of an initiative, to set goals and agree on strategies and tactics, and to pinpoint how to measure outcomes—well, that can be the difference between a company being an average performer in its market and achieving elite status."

Sean and Mike agree on a timeline for launching the top three initiatives they've identified and set a date a couple weeks out to "close the loop" on their Learning Loop overview by applying the final component of the process. That will also be a good time to review how Mike has applied the first four components to the new initiatives and the performance of his sales team.

Over the next two work days, Mike gathers information, consults with colleagues, and refines the planning document for the new application process (Figure 7.3). When it is ready to go, he attaches it with an invitation for the initial planning meeting with representatives from Sales, Operations, Finance, and IT. He leans back in his chair, closes his eyes, and lets out a sigh as he reflects on a busy and productive six days. Then his eyes snap open again as he realizes it has been just a week and a day since he sat at this desk reviewing sales reports with something close to despair. Mike reaches for his journal to reflect in written form about what a difference those six days have meant for his outlook, his approach to work, and his hopes for the future. Ending each day by reviewing his journal entries and adding new thoughts has already become a comfortable routine.

Summary of Key Concepts

- **Show Me, Don't Tell Me.** Department, division, and enterprise plans are committed to document form. The effort required to create written plans engages a different level of thinking, moving from high-level strategy to tactics that can be implemented. Reality testing comes through this process as leaders discover key links to solid execution. Standardization of templates, forms, and other tools are leaders' responsibility, thereby creating a common lexicon/language and in the process facilitating greater synergy among stakeholders.

- **Purpose, S.M.A.R.T. Goals, Strategies, Tactics, and Outcomes.** Cascading ideas to implementable steps clear to all stakeholders requires a continuum of thought covering answers to the questions of

INITIATIVE: NEW INSURANCE APPLICATION PROCESS

CHAMPIONS

The leaders who are ultimately responsible for achieving outcomes.

Mike Spur, Regional Sales Manager
Sean McCarthy, National Sales Manager

PURPOSE

The deepest reason for the initiative. The purpose statement drives the development of strategy, tactics, and outcomes. A purpose, however, is not achieved but instead is pursued every day.

Develop a new insurance application process that improves the experience for key stakeholders (e.g., clients, sales agents, operations, etc.).

GOALS

These are the categories of achievement that must be obtained in order to achieve our purpose / aim. Our goals are SMART:

    S - Specific
    M - Measurable
    A - Attainable
    R - Realistic
    T - Timely

DEFINITION *A goal is an observable and measurable end result having one or more objectives to be achieved within a more or less fixed timeframe.*

1. Determine whether TCI should build or buy new application process. Present recommendation to Board of Directors for approval no later than December 31, 2016.

2. Increase stakeholders satisfaction (see above) with the process by 20% no later than 6 months after implementation.

3. Increase the effectiveness of the process as measured by application / policy delivered ratio by 10% no later than 6 months after implementation.

STRATEGIES

Our plans of action that will help us achieve our goals.

DEFINITION *A plan of action to achieve a goal.*

Establish a team to research and develop TCI's new insurance application process. The senior managers assigned as the core team members are: Mike Spur (Lead) and Sean McCarthy. These leaders are delegated broad powers in order to develop a plan. Other members of management, Operations, Information Technology, etc., may participate in the planning process in order to develop the plan to be approved by TCI's Board of Directors before implementation by the core team.

TACTICS

Concrete ways that we implement our strategies.

DEFINITION *Systematic determination and scheduling of immediate or short-term activities required in achieving the objectives of strategic planning.*

The tactics (illustrative examples only) that support our strategies:

1. Establish an "Agent Advisory Council" to ensure the new process includes their inputs.

2. Hold focus groups with valued clients.

3. Provide incentives for clients who will use the self-service delivery channel.

OUTCOMES

Measures that help us determine whether we are achieving our purpose so that we stay focused on what was intended. To accomplish this, measures are articulated as short-term and long-term as well as qualitative and quantitative data points from multiple viewing points, thereby providing a holistic view.

	SHORT-TERM *within six months*	LONG-TERM *beyond six months*
	FREQUENCY | CHAMPION	FREQUENCY | CHAMPION
QUALITATIVE		
Client Focus Groups	Quarterly Sean	Quarterly Sean
Agent Focus Groups	Quarterly Mike	Quarterly Mike
QUANTITATIVE		
Application / Policy Ratio	Daily Mike	Daily Mike
% of clients using self-service	Daily Mike *(establish baseline)*	Daily Mike
Client Satisfaction Survey	Monthly Mike	Monthly Mike

Figure 7.3 Completed Planning Document

why, what, whom, how, when, and how we measure. Leadership that tasks the team to work without first fleshing out these particulars is underdeveloped at best. The process of formulating purpose, goals, strategies, tactics, and targeted outcomes is most effectively done with high stakeholder involvement and through group dialogue with several aims, including buy-in, clarification, iteration, and calibration of each stakeholder's grasp of the work ahead.

- **Accountability and Clarity.** What must be done, by whom, and by when? Teamwork succeeds when a captain is steering the ship: Leaders must know when to inspect and validate whether their teams are on course—and do so at intervals that allow timely course correction. It's crucial to know the causal link between activities and results and to demonstrate understanding, accountability, and ownership.

Chapter 8

What Did We Learn?

Mike heads down the hallway to the conference room for what Sean has dubbed his "Learning Loop debrief."

Over the past two weeks, this stroll has become routine for Mike. Between team planning sessions and meetings with the vendor on the new application process and the launch of the biweekly sessions of sales agents and operations specialists, Mike feels as if he's spent more time in the conference room than in his own office. Not that he's complaining. Most of the time he has spent at that table has been extremely productive—even energizing—and the initiatives he is leading are well underway.

Sales for his team are trending up, too, even before the launch of the new app. Rather than responding to the sessions with Operations, which have been nicknamed "Go Team meetings," with groans, his agents embraced the idea and seem to have come away from the first session enthusiastic and ready to apply practical ideas for increasing applications and turning applications into policies.

Mike is not surprised when he enters the conference room to see four familiar faces around the table. Sean is chatting with Nikki, while Phil and Sammy are deep in discussion, peering at the screen of the laptop open between them. All of them look up with smiles as Mike takes a seat at the table.

"Before we dig in, I want to thank you all for your support and willingness to share your know-how with me," Mike says. "The last few weeks have reminded me of all the concrete ways that TCI's vision to help customers thrive also applies to the people who work here."

"Hear, hear!" Nikki chimes in. "The supportive environment here really is TCI's secret sauce. It's hard to put into words what a difference it makes to work for a company that cares about its staff."

"Organizations that don't support their employees have a hard time fulfilling their mission to customers," Sammy says softly. "But I think that each of us here knows first-hand that Jim McKinnon takes an interest in his staff's success that goes beyond a means to the ends of increased sales. He was my first mentor, and working at TCI introduced me to many of the principles in the Learning Loop."

"And you returned the favor by reminding us of those principles a few years back," Phil says. "Your consulting work with the firm really helped TCI get back on track."

"There is a saying that what goes around comes around," Sammy says. "I believe it is usually applied to ill feelings, but in this case it sums up my delight in being able to help out a company that was so important to my career."

Sammy moves to the whiteboard. "Mike, I believe that your experience over these last few weeks is a microcosm of how TCI regained its bearing and focus on doing what matters," he says. "And like the company, I believe you will find the Learning Loop to be a useful framework going forward. It describes a recursive, continual process of monitoring what is going on, staying grounded in what really matters, considering your options for growing the business, and carefully planning and implementing the course you've identified."

As Sammy points out each of the components, Mike notices for the first time that each entry in the Learning Loop is connected to the next with an arrow to represent a continuous cycle. He realizes that the name of the framework isn't just alliterative but representative of that cycle. "Now I get why it's a loop," Mike says out loud, as the others nod and grin.

"Precisely," Sammy says. "And that's why this fifth component, What did we learn?, is not the end of the process, but simply the next step in reflecting on what has been implemented, how performance is going, and what corrections might be in order.

"I know your work on the new application process is still underway, but you've had your first meeting with your sales team and Operations," he continues. "How did that go?"

"It went really well," Mike says. "I expected some reluctance on both sides, but my agents seemed very open about the opportunity to meet with the operations team, and vice versa. There were lots of good ideas, and we even came up with agendas for our next two meetings."

Sean joins in. "A couple of the Ops folks stopped by my office to suggest that the other sales teams might benefit from similar meetings, so we're looking into that. I know you've just had the one meeting, but do you have any thoughts on changes down the road?"

Mike thinks for a moment. "Well, after a couple more meetings with Ops, I was thinking about inviting representatives from Finance to share their ideas and perspectives. And I want to keep a close eye on the exchanges around the table. If it starts to feel flat or less productive down the road, we might be better off going to monthly meetings.

"But I think there will be some value in repetition—of Operations driving home key points about the best ways to work with the various carriers and the features and benefits of new and popular products," he adds. "Our newer agents need to be steeped in those kinds of details, but I think it will be helpful for the veteran salespeople, too."

"In my line of work, we call that inculcated knowledge, Mike," Sammy says, "meaning that the most important aspects of one's work are often learned through repeated exposure and practice. And, yes, even for long-time professionals, reminders are helpful."

Sammy turns to the whiteboard and writes "Learning Loop's Purpose" next to the fifth component on the diagram, What did we learn? He explains that several elements central to optimizing the utility of the Learning Loop at this stage are purposefully engaging in self-reflection, identifying corrective action, creating opportunities to emphasize essential knowledge, and, when necessary, conducting "autopsies" of initiatives that go off track and processes and procedures that may need to be updated or overhauled.

"And don't forget celebrating!" Phil says. "That was one of the things I learned from Jim early on—how important it is to recognize and celebrate progress. I remember walking into the office at lunchtime one day to find everybody from Finance and Ops having a pizza party. Jim invited me to join in the celebration for the successful implementation of new accounting software. I thought that was a little overboard, but when one of the financial analysts showed me all the reporting capabilities, I could see how it would improve efficiency. And she, and everybody there, really was excited and pleased about how well it all went, so, yeah, I could understand why a celebration was in order."

"That's just part of our culture, I think," Sean says. "We encourage everyone to be objective about how they are performing and how the company's doing, so that we all gently guide ourselves and each other to do the best we can. So, of course, we celebrate each other's successes as well."

Sammy nods in agreement. "This shared attitude helps to foster continual progress along a trajectory that reenergizes the organization on a regular basis. I've worked with other companies where the corporate attitude is brash, even abrasive, and it's like everyone is just looking out for themselves. That outlook only gets you so far before everything starts to break down."

The executive team at TCI, led by Jim McKinnon, decided early on to foster a different kind of culture, powered by the principles represented in the Learning Loop, he continues. Sammy suggests that his listeners picture a flywheel with five handles, representing each of the five steps involved in doing what matters. Now imagine that each time the team gets a good grip on one of these handles and pushes the flywheel forward, it gains momentum.

Failure to perform one of the five steps decreases the speed of the flywheel. For example, inadequate research, a less-than-optimal array of options, or failure to develop S.M.A.R.T. goals could slow organizational progress. But when the team works together to perform each step with greater mastery, the enterprise moves along at a productive clip. Because each stakeholder has a hand on the flywheel, all must understand the five steps and participate fully to create harmony within the ecosystem. This is full potential. The leader's job is to set the flywheel into motion and guide stakeholders to understand and do their part.

"When everyone believes—and acts on their belief—that everyone contributes, then everyone wins. We know this in our heads, in our hearts, and in our guts. This is the highest expression of Doing What Matters," Sammy concludes. "And when this outlook is shared across the organization, the result is continual progress that is wiser, more cohesive, and more confident. The enterprise is continually moving from current state to future state. When it does so by adhering to each step in the Learning Loop, it progresses with greater effect because it is building on previous gains."

He turns back to the whiteboard and adds one more entry next to the Learning Loop, "Assessment and Evaluation" (see Figure 8.1).

Figure 8.1 The Learning Loop Component 5: What did we learn?

"Now I need a refresher," Nikki admits. "I know there is a difference between assessment and evaluation, but like most people, I think, I use these terms interchangeably."

In everyday use, Sammy responds, these words might be more or less synonymous, but in the context of the Learning Loop, there are some key distinctions. "As we define it, assessing is an approach to determine what is going on without affixing value, good or bad, right or wrong, and without personal biases. The more viewing points that a leader can harvest, the greater potential to optimize learning," he says. "The central question becomes: What did we learn, and how does that inform future decisions about people, process, and technology?"

Evaluation, on the other hand, seeks to measure where we stand in relation to what we had hoped to achieve, he explains. It is more quantitative, measured by metrics such as return on investment, impact on budget, and scheduling and quality benchmarks.

Both assessment and evaluation are essential in optimizing the Learning Loop, Sammy continues. Evaluation is often used for peer-to-peer analysis, performance appraisals, incentive programs, and bonus awards. Proper delegation at the planning and implementation stage contributes significantly to effective evaluation. Leaders should be clear when they are in assessing/learning mode vs. evaluating/benchmarking mode. Assessment can be energizing while evaluation can consume energy, but there is a time and place for both.

"It's like inhaling and exhaling—we need both to thrive," he concludes. "Sophisticated leaders understand the differences and apply the right approach at the right time."

"Well, I may need a little more help developing my level of sophisticated leadership," Mike says with a laugh, "but I do feel like I'm making good progress, and with your useful input today, I'll be able to keep the Learning Loop rolling."

In the evening, after tucking the kids in, Mike and Megan collapse contentedly on the sofa, and Mike recounts his final meeting with the group who introduced him to a process and principles he has found useful in every aspect of his work. Megan, who has been paging through Mike's journal as he talks, stops at the page where he has sketched in the Learning Loop diagram. She traces the diagram with one finger and then stops on the "What are our options?" component, tapping it thoughtfully.

"You know, I've been thinking about applying this loop to my own pursuits," Megan says. "Now that both kids are in school, I've been thinking about getting back into marketing."

"You mean, going back to your old firm?" Mike asks. "Your boss said she'd welcome you back whenever you were ready."

"Actually, I've been thinking about doing some consulting on my own. I have a couple friends running businesses who are constantly running their marketing ideas by me. And my work on the marketing committee of the community foundation may result in some leads, too."

Megan explains that she's been working through the Learning Loop step by step, figuring out how many hours she could devote to launching a business on a weekly basis and what she'd need to set up shop; identifying potential clients; studying local market conditions; and taking an objective view of how marketing has changed since she left her full-time job several years ago. In preparation, she's decided to enroll in a continuing education course at the local university on social media marketing.

"Social media wasn't really in the picture as a marketing tool back then. But now?" she says, and Mike can hear the excitement in her voice. "I've been using Facebook and Pinterest, but I need to immerse myself in learning how to deploy them as business tools."

"This is awesome," Mike tells Megan. "I know you've been thinking about getting back into marketing, but I didn't realize how extensive your planning's been."

"I'd just been tossing the idea around until you started talking about this whole Learning Loop concept," she says. "First, I got to thinking about how we could apply the process in planning our financial goals, but then I realized it could really help me more deliberately explore this idea of launching a consulting business."

Megan and Mike talk late into the night about her plans, his work, and their goals for their family—doing what matters for themselves and their children. Only when the clock on the mantle chimes do they look up simultaneously and realize that it is midnight. "What matters right now is getting some sleep," Mike says ruefully.

"You go ahead, honey. I'll be there in a minute," Megan murmurs as she jots a few more notes about business ideas on her iPad.

Summary of Key Concepts

- **Optimizing the Learning Loop.** Self-reflection, corrective action, inculcated knowledge, celebration, and autopsies are among the tools that give the Learning Loop its cyclical nature. Wielding these tools allows a culture to objectively view itself and gently fosters continual progress that is wiser, more cohesive, and more confident, powering a performance trajectory that regularly reenergizes the enterprise. Moving from current state to future state, from point A to point B, is recursive and repeats with greater effect if the enterprise adheres to each step in the Learning Loop.

- **Assessment and Evaluation.** Assessing is an approach to determine what is going on without affixing value, good or bad, right or wrong, and without personal biases. The more viewing points that a leader can harvest, the greater potential for learning. The central question is: What did we learn, and how does that inform future decisions about people, process, and technology? Evaluation, on the other hand, seeks to measure where we stand in relation to what we had hoped to achieve (e.g., return on investment, on budget, on quality). Both assessment and evaluation are essential in optimizing the Learning Loop.

Chapter 9

Doing What Matters at Work and in Life

"I think she's discovered her true passion," Mike says wryly.

Mr. McKinnon follows Mike's gaze—and laughs out loud. Mike's daughter, Jessica, is wielding a shovel as if she was born to the work of mucking out a stall, all the while chatting excitedly with Kate McKinnon about the horses.

"Kate has this saying: 'If you love even the dirty work, then you're a horse person,'" her husband recounts fondly. "So, yes, I'd say your daughter has caught the bug."

Mike sighs in mock resignation. "I guess we'd better give her a choice between swim camp and riding camp next summer, but it doesn't look like swim camp's going to stand much of a chance."

They stand in a comfortable silence, surveying the scene of the annual TCI holiday gathering at the McKinnon ranch. It is a warm, sunny Saturday in mid-December, and employees and spouses chat animatedly under and around a large awning sheltering tables being set for dinner as their children join in yard games and line up for horse rides.

Kate and Jessica are joined by a teenaged girl who reaches up to tousle the forelock of a horse in the next stall. "I guess I should have warned you, Mike, about the lure of the McKinnon horse barn for girls of a certain age," says Sean, as he joins the two men. "Our Cassie competes in dressage, and it all started when Kate took her on a barn tour ... oh, it must have been eight years ago now."

Switching gears, Sean says, "I know this is a party, but I did want to mention that I called up the login data and application rates for the first two weeks of agents beta-testing the new app. Cassie wanted to practice driving, and her mother volunteered to ride shotgun, so I had to do something in the backseat to occupy my time. Anyway, the numbers are looking great, and the feedback from agents has been awesome."

"So we'll be ready to roll it out for customers the first of the year?" Mr. McKinnon says.

"Right on schedule," Mike agrees. "And even though that's what we planned in our first meetings with SCI, I will admit I'm a little surprised—and very pleased—that we've been able to keep the project on track."

"All that up-front planning paid off, right?" Sean says. "Steve was telling me last week that the Ops team involved in implementation had their doubts about the timeline initially, but everyone has been pleasantly surprised with how well it came together and how well the app has been delivering on expectations."

"It sounds like someone is talking business," says Nikki, who is navigating the wheelchair of a smiling, older woman, "so I feel comfortable interrupting to introduce you to my mother, Annika Jenkins."

Nikki completes the introductions, and Mrs. Jenkins extends her hand to shake with each of the three men. She continues to hold Mr. McKinnon's hand as she thanks him for his hospitality. "I think my Nikki is very lucky to have you for her boss," she tells him. "Her father was in the insurance business, too, and oh, he worked such long hours. But Nikki, she walks in my front door every day by 6—and tells me, 'Don't worry, Ma, I'm doing fine at work.'"

"Better than fine, Mrs. Jenkins—your daughter is one of our top agents," Mike tells her. "You should be very proud."

Mrs. Jenkins reaches to pat the hand her daughter has placed on her shoulder and beams up at Nikki. As he watches the fond moment between mother and daughter, Sean notices a familiar face in the background. "Wait," he says, "is that Maria Cortez?"

"Indeed it is," Mike says. "So you recognize the newest member of my sales team?"

Maria was one of the first people Mike met on his "field assignments" to discover how to apply the Learning Loop to improve his sales team's performance. In their meeting, she suggested that TCI consider signing on with her company, Southern California Insurance, to license its automated application processing software. And when TCI did so, Maria accepted Mike's offer of employment, looking forward to working in a sales territory closer to her home.

As if sensing their eyes upon her, Maria looks up and approaches the group. She says hello to her old friend, Nikki, and new boss, Mike, and introduces herself formally to Sean and Mr. McKinnon. "Thanks for inviting me to this party, even though I won't be moving to TCI until the new year," she tells Mr. McKinnon. "It's a great way to meet my new coworkers informally and to see for myself TCI's reputation for taking care of its people."

"We're glad you could join us," Mr. McKinnon says warmly. "And I hope you will see over time that Tri Counties Insurance thrives by helping its employees to thrive—and that's not just an empty slogan."

"That's why I'm here," Maria says. "A shorter commute is certainly part of it, but I've also heard such great things from Nikki about your organization over the years. And I have to say I was impressed by how quickly and efficiently your company transitioned to the new application process."

"I understand that we have you to thank for the initial suggestion," Mr. McKinnon says. "I look forward to meeting you again as you get settled in at TCI. I want to learn about your personal and professional goals. But now it looks like it's time to sound the dinner bell."

Maria joins Mike at a long table with several other agents on his team and their families. She finds herself seated next to Tim Gerard, who introduces himself and welcomes her to the team. He talks enthusiastically about the new app and the positive impact it has had on his sales ratios. Though Tim is the rookie agent in the San Diego County region, he is also one of the most technologically adept and thus has adapted quickly to using the new automated system. In fact, several of his colleagues have relied on Tim for guidance in using the new app.

Across the table, Mike observes as Tim and Maria compare notes on using the application system with clients. Mike has been pleased to see Tim's self-confidence and enthusiasm for his work increase in recent weeks. In fact, Tim's willingness to work with some of his colleagues who had reservations about the new system has helped to enhance the performance of the entire team.

Megan is seated just down the table from Mike, with their two children between them, and is chatting pleasantly with Sammy Tanaka. From the lilt in her voice, Mike can tell she is talking about the plans for her new business. But most of his attention is occupied by Jessica, seated next to him, talking with exhilaration about Kate McKinnon's invitation to return to the ranch over the holiday break to go riding. Mike listens with one ear as he is suddenly struck by a realization: Has it only been three months since I sat at my desk, feeling desperate and bewildered? I felt like I was on the brink of failure and had no idea how to turn things around. But I did—with the help of so many people here today.

The dinner ends with warm words from Mr. McKinnon for all of his employees. With an upswing in sales in the fourth quarter, TCI is on track for a record year. "The numbers are great," the CEO tells his staff and their families, "but what matters more is how each of you contributed to help us realize our commitment to help our policy-holders thrive."

He shares several examples of that commitment in action. Two agents on Mike's team are working with low- to moderate-income families who qualify for mortgages through a community program to obtain the homeowners' coverage they need. An agent in the Orange County region set up an office in a business incubator center to consult with fledgling entrepreneurs on their companies' insurance options. Nikki has been leading workshops for retirees who belong to a local credit union on their changing insurance needs and options, and she is developing an in-house training for agents on that topic.

Mr. McKinnon ends with a salute to Mike Spur for leading the initiative for the new automated application software—and to TCI's newest agent, Maria Cortez, for the initial suggestion about partnering with SCI. "We have always prided ourselves on our personal approach to serving our customers and have taken a more deliberate approach to technology investments," Mr. McKinnon concludes. "We believe that this new system will bring us closer to our clients and their expectations for quick and efficient service, so now we can spend more time talking with them about their needs and less time filling out forms and waiting for approvals from our carriers."

His comments are met with thunderous applause, and Mike is pleased to see a couple of his agents who were apprehensive about the new system actually on their feet leading the ovation. He joins them and raises his glass in a gesture of toasting his team gathered round the table.

As the party draws to a close, Mike and Megan make the rounds, extending holiday wishes to each of Mike's agents and his or her family in turn. Then Megan works her way over to the McCarthys, and Mike knows she will be thanking Sean for his continued support. Since the early days of Mike's career with TCI, the McCarthys have been good friends, and Mike has shared with Megan his gratitude for Sean's guidance in recent months.

Mike turns to find Sammy by his side. "Happy holidays to one of my favorite Fellow Learners," Mike says, echoing a phrase that Sammy used in one of their Learning Loop sessions.

Sammy smiles and bows slightly. "And best wishes to an avid learner," he responds. "I see and hear that you are putting the principles we discussed into practice to great impact for TCI—and you have been sharing them at home as well?"

"Yes, I thought Megan might be talking with you over dinner about her own application of the Learning Loop."

"Indeed. Her enthusiasm for her work is quite compelling. I understand she may be leaving this party with a new client on board. Kate McKinnon is interested in consulting with Megan on promoting a scholarship fundraiser."

Mike laughs as Jessica and Jake run up, begging for one last visit to the barn to say good night to the horses. Seeing that Megan is still deep in conversation with Sean and his wife, Mike acquiesces.

Mr. McKinnon finds Mike and his children near the horse stalls. As Jake and Jessica coo softly to the large animals, Mike tells his boss and host, "I was just remembering my last visit to the ranch and trying to find the right words to tell you what a great mentor you were that day—and throughout my years with the company, actually."

"No need," Mr. McKinnon says. "I appreciate that you've always given TCI your full effort. Sure, you've had some tough spots. Who hasn't? But I've never had the sense that you're just—what's that saying?— phoning it in. TCI thrives because people like you lead with your head and with your heart."

"It means a lot to me for you to say that," Mike says sincerely, "but really, I've just been following your example and trying to get better at this leadership business every day."

"Walk, trot, canter, right, Mike?" Mr. McKinnon says, and Jessica looks up curiously.

"Dad, are you going for a horse ride, too?" she asks.

"No, honey, I think I'll leave that to you," he says with a laugh. "But for now, I think we'd better let the horses rest and go find your mother."

Conclusion

We all need a champion, someone who sees our potential—sometimes before we see it in ourselves. Among the responsibilities of a leader is to promote the development of others by providing the resources and environment in which people can learn, grow, and realize their full capacity for achievement. A greater percentage of employees working at or near their full potential propels the organization forward. Employees are rewarded with opportunities for advancement, monetary gains, and recognition for their contributions, and the enterprise benefits from their combined, continuing advances.

When leaders embrace this approach—and enlightened executives do—they establish a strong foundation for their organizations. But these leaders need a champion as well. The full potential of an enterprise is realized when its C-suite inhabitants are supported by a community of like-minded leaders.

Sustaining this dynamic requires that executives, who are the stewards of capital, including human capital, embrace their responsibility for building communities in which personal development is an expectation that is fostered and rewarded. Top executives should be the sponsors, architects, and builders of leadership development programs. This is not a responsibility that can be delegated or handled in a perfunctory manner.

Doing What Matters chronicles how one organization strives to build leaders. This story is not intended as an organizational blueprint. Each enterprise has its own personality and philosophy, but as diverse as they may be, successful companies have several attributes in common, including a commitment to support leadership development. I hope the concepts outlined in this book enlighten leaders about different approaches for developing their own leadership community and inspire them to take bold action.

As a step in that direction, I invite you to complete the following assessment on key dimensions of a strong leadership community. The results of this assessment can be used to ignite crucial dialogue about ways to strengthen leadership development in your organization. Good luck!

Instructions for
Doing What Matters | Organizational Assessment

To get a sense of your organization's effectiveness, complete this assessment by rating your strengths on a scale of 1 to 5 in the areas outlined on the following page. Simply place a dot on the grid where your answer (1-5) intersects with the question that you are rating. Then, turn the page to a landscape (horizontal) position, and connect the dots with a heavy line, thereby creating a graph. In what areas do you find opportunities for improvement?

Doing What Matters | Organizational Assessment

How well does our organization ...	Poor Performer	Below Average Performer	Average Performer	Nearing Benchmark Status	Benchmark Status
Champion leaders (e.g., our Mike Spurs) in an effort to improve their performance and help them thrive?					
Involve senior leaders (e.g., Jim McKinnon, Sean McCarthy) in developing the next generation of leaders?					
Use our vision, mission, and core values (e.g., Figure 3.1) as a filter to align our business plans?					
Teach a shared process (e.g., Figure 3.1) for assessing what is going on in order to drive performance?					
Use a combination of data (e.g., qualitative, quantitative, outside-in, inside-out) to create holistic views (Figure 4.2) of the way things really are?					
Leverage outside mentors (e.g., Sammy Tanaka) in developing the next generation of leaders?					
Champion processes (e.g., journaling, cave time) for reflection, thinking, and planning?					
Break down high-level initiatives into easily understood plans (e.g., Figure 7.3)?					
Take the time to learn staffs' personal and professional goals (e.g., Nikki's need for a regular schedule)?					
Set the right "tension" for our growth trajectory (e.g., Figure 6.2)?					
Identify and vet all possible options before anchoring on "one right answer" (e.g., Figure 7.2)?					
Differentiate between purpose, goals, strategies, tactics, and outcomes (e.g., Figure 7.3)?					
Create clarity and accountability (e.g., Figure 7.3) for outcomes on business measures as well as projects?					
Take the time to reflect to learn and grow in effort to thrive?					

Acknowledgments

Doing What Matters chronicles the commitment of colleagues and family members to champion the main character's resurgence through life's felt difficulties. Like Mike Spur, I've been blessed with champions whose incredible support has made all the difference in my professional and personal life. Their positive influence has helped me shape the principles central to this book.

Mike Steinhour at Valley Federal Savings was the first person to see my potential in the financial services industry. I am grateful for the countless hours he spent sharing his knowledge about the insurance business. Dr. John Langevin coached me through incredible felt difficulties of a layoff early in my career. Phil Hart at Logix (formerly Lockheed Federal Credit Union) introduced me to the credit union business and, more importantly, championed my advancement into senior management with concrete lessons about what it means to be an executive.

As the CFO at Fox Entertainment, Dean Hallet modeled for this newly minted CEO what leadership grace in a boardroom looks like. Dr. David Burger served as my executive coach over eight years, helping me to hone a leadership approach based on ecocentric leadership principles integrating head and heart. Finally, my thanks to the staff, management, and volunteers of Partners Federal Credit Union for collectively challenging me to learn and grow every day.

As I worked on this book, I relied on Karen Bankston of Precision Prose (precision-prose.com) for editing and guidance through what initially seemed a daunting challenge of production and publication. Thanks to Lorraine Ortner-Blake (lorraineortner-blake.com) for designing the cover and graphics that illustrate the core concepts of *Doing What Matters*. In addition, I appreciate the work of Web developer Charles Jones (charlesajones.com) in designing The CEO Corner website to showcase its content and to make it easy for users to navigate.

Many thanks to my colleagues and associates who took the time to review a first draft of this work and provide valuable feedback: Gary Ahlgren, Dr. David Burger, Dr. Susan Cain, Jim Kasch, Bill Partin, Gene Pelham, and John Tippets.

The most important people in my life also helped shape this book. I thank John and Shirley Janclaes for the blessing of seven siblings and for their dedication in teaching us how to love and support one another. My daughters Jillian and Lindsey have provided for some of the brightest moments of my life. Jackie Real-Salas, my wife and soulmate of 15 years, has never wavered in her support of me pursuing my dreams.

About the Author

John Janclaes has more than thirty years of experience in the financial services industry, spanning retail banking, brokerage, and insurance. He joined Partners Federal Credit Union in June 2004 as President and Chief Executive Officer. With eleven branches located primarily in California and Florida, Partners serves employees of the The Walt Disney Company, currently numbering more than 125,000 members with $1.4 billion in assets under management.

Previously, John was an executive with Logix (formerly Lockheed Federal Credit Union), where he served in a number of executive roles, including Senior Vice President, Chief Business Development Officer, and Vice President of Lending.

He also worked for Duerr Financial, Coast Federal Bank, and Valley Federal Savings.

As an advocate for the credit union movement, John is called on regularly to speak at industry events and to serve in an advisory capacity for trade association groups, including the National Association of Federal Credit Unions (NAFCU), Credit Union National Association (CUNA), and Filene Research Institute, a financial services think tank. He has been honored with the James D. Likens Award as a distinguished alumnus of the Western CUNA Management School, where he now volunteers on the Board of Trustees.

John contributes to the communities in which he works and lives by serving as one of the founding Board Members for L.E.T.M.S.A.I.L., a nonprofit organization serving adults with mental disabilities. He is also the Executive Champion for the Southern California Special Olympics, for which he was named Executive Volunteer of the Year for The Walt Disney Company.

A native of California, John holds a bachelor's degree in business administration from the University of Redlands, a master's in business management from Claremont College, and numerous professional designations. He currently resides in Temecula, California, with his wife, Jackie, where they pursue their passion for equestrian sports.

John is founder of The CEO Corner, an online forum to help business leaders and their organizations thrive (www.theceocorner.com). In recognition of John's commitment to leadership development, proceeds from the sale of this book will be donated to support scholarships and coaching for business leaders in training.

Made in the USA
San Bernardino, CA
11 September 2017